I0071593

# Start Your Own Travel Agency

by
Adam Starchild

**Books for Business**
**New York - Hong Kong**

Start Your Own Travel Agency

by
Adam Starchild

ISBN: 0-89499-236-8

Copyright © 2000 by Adam Starchild

Books for Business
New York - Hong Kong
http://www.BusinessBooksInternational.com

All rights reserved, including the right to reproduce
this book, or portions thereof, in any form.

# Contents

# Introduction

Travel and tourism is one of the fastest growing industries in the world. Occupying a vast sector of the economy, the industry is comprised of countless individuals and companies that provide a wide assortment of services to travelers. With the number of travelers increasing annually throughout the world, it is expected that the travel and tourism sector will continue to expand.

When people travel for pleasure or business, most turn to travel agents to help them plan their trips. Thus, the travel agent is at the hub of the industry. It is the travel agent who guides travelers through the maze of choices for transportation, accommodations, tours, and rentals. While the Internet enjoys much press for the alternatives it offers to travelers who wish to book their own flights and hotels, the fact is that travel agents in the United States alone account for the sale of three out of every four airline tickets and the sale of nine out of ten cruise packages. In 1999, U.S. travel agencies accounted for close to $50 billion in ticket sales.

The future for the travel and tourism industry is bright. Currently the industry ranks as the second largest business enterprise in the U.S., and many economists expect that it will soon become the largest. The industry accounts for 6.7 of America's GNP, and this, too, is likely to grow. The reasons for this are varied and include:

- The world is getting smaller. Modern transportation systems reach into every corner of the globe, making it easier to visit places that just a few years ago would have been nearly impossible to visit.

- More countries than ever welcome tourists because of the economic benefits they bring. Many countries that not long ago had closed borders are now open and eager for tourist dollars.

- The decade of the nineties witnessed significant worldwide economic expansion, which increased the disposable income for millions of families. This is particularly true of Western nations and Japan.

- The aging baby boomer population of the U.S. – those individuals between the ages of 46 and 54 – is at the peak of its earning power. Moreover, in many of these families, children are grown and have finished college, leaving their parents with new-found income and wealth. A big part of this wealth is used for travel. Indeed, American baby boomers are among the most active groups in the travel and tourism industry.

• Retired individuals account for a large part of the travel industry's revenues. Free from the responsibilities of raising children and building careers, many retired people regularly travel to places they always wanted to visit but previously did not have the time or money. Given the fact that America's population, as well as the populations of Western Europe and Japan, are graying, it is likely that "seniors" will continue to help fuel the travel industry's expansion.

All this bodes particularly well for travel agents and their agencies. Although the industry is highly competitive, hard-working travel agents enjoy great success. Aside from the pleasure of operating a successful business, there are many other opportunities that one may realize as a travel agent. Many of these opportunities are rather common, cited regularly in travel articles. Impressive discounts, complimentary accommodations, and free tours are typical, but there is much more for the travel agent who also views himself as an entrepreneur.

The creative travel agent does not limit himself to simply booking trips for others, but uses his position as a springboard for taking advantage of global opportunities. For example, when taking advantage of a free (or very low cost) *familiarization* tour of Europe – sponsored by a tour operator to acquaint agents with his itinerary – a travel agent may use his down time to explore business opportunities in the region. There may be local companies in which he may wish to invest, he may find that he can establish a tour for a niche market, or he may find through first-hand experience that the host country's laws will enable him to invest in foreign securities at substantial tax savings. Opportunities abound for those who are willing to find them.

The closing years of the millennium have witnessed a revolution in the travel industry. In the past, the industry was filled with companies that maintained storefront offices. Indeed, some travel agencies maintained several offices. This is no longer true. While the offices still exist, the technological revolution has enabled many travel agents to work out of their homes, freeing them from the need of maintaining a large office with expensive overhead. A small room, a moderately priced computer and Internet connection, phone system, desk and chair are often all that is needed to conduct travel business from one's home-based office.

The industry has become open to virtually anyone who loves travel and embraces the challenge of owning a business. Using his phone and computer, the agent working from his home can easily book airlines, cruises, hotels, and tours, working when and as much as he or she likes. Some people become travel agents to establish a home business that will become their career, but many others prefer to work only part-time as travel agents. Whatever way you choose to operate your travel business, you still can enjoy all of the many benefits, prestige, and success that come with being a travel agent.

Individuals who are interested in becoming travel agents should not simply accept the traditional bounds and benefits that come with travel agencies, chiefly the booking of trips and the chance to travel cheaply themselves, but should look upon the many global opportunities that they can enjoy. While they should view themselves as travel agents, they should also view themselves as entrepreneurs.

Of course, to realize the many opportunities that will be available to you, you will need to keep your mind and eyes open, be willing to investigate and pursue alternatives for possible investment, and accept that hard work is essential to being successful in an increasingly competitive world. However, if you enjoy traveling at little or no cost, desire to own and operate a business, and wish to pursue investments and business opportunities on a global scale, becoming a travel agent is one of the most effective methods of attaining your goals.

# The Challenge and Benefits of Becoming a Travel Agent

While just about everybody knows what a travel agent is, few people outside of the industry actually know all that a travel agent does. Without question it is job that requires various skills but also offers excellent rewards and benefits. Along with realizing the satisfaction of arranging trips for people, travel agents can travel the world at deeply reduced costs. The also have the potential to earn an excellent income and enjoy the numerous advantages – most importantly tax benefits – that come with owning a business.

As a travel agent, your days and tasks will be varied. In the course of your day you might be making flight and hotel reservations for a business traveler, book a white-water rapids vacation in Colorado for a family, or arrange a tour of Europe for the German club of your local high school. You may explain the customs and visa requirements of a country of the Far East to a client, offer suggestions to a retired couple as to what clothes to pack for a trip to Ireland, or provide information about the best hotels to stay in during a visit to San Francisco.

To do all this, you will need various skills, particularly those that enable you to deal effectively with people. Successful travel agents usually possess most or all of the following traits:

- A good understanding of operating a business.

- General knowledge about the world and specific knowledge about travel.

- The ability to promote and sell services.

- The ability to explain information clearly to others.

- The ability to use reference and resource materials and directories.

- The ability to utilize computers to optimize operations.

- An enjoyment of working with and conversing with others.

- The desire to satisfy clients.

In addition, successful travel agents possess many of the traits common to entrepreneurs. Successful travel agents are:

- Motivated to succeed.

- Goal-oriented.

- Creative.

- Able to find and recognize new ideas.

- Open-minded and willing to look at situations from various angles.

- Able to assess situations and conditions accurately.

- Persevering.

- Determined.

- Able to make decisions.

- Willing to take calculated risks.

- Well organized.

- Able to communicate easily and express ideas clearly.

- Self-confident, but not overconfident.

- Able to adapt to changing conditions.

- Able to inspire others.

The travel industry is vibrant and dynamic. More than ever people are traveling the world over for business and pleasure. The industry is growing and the need for competent agents is high. If you like to travel, would like to establish your own business, and wish to explore the world as an entrepreneur seeking investment opportunities, becoming a travel agent can be the first step to achieving your goals.

# A Brief History of the Travel Industry

The travel industry no doubt has its origins well back in history. It is likely that enterprising individuals in ancient civilizations arranged for the travel of others. Unfortunately, there are no surviving records of such "agencies."

The first travel agency of which evidence exists is that of Thomas Cook, a Englishman, who by 1845 had established a business to arrange trips for travelers. Recognizing the need of travelers for help in planning their trips, Cook soon began booking ocean voyages and hotel accommodations and eventually developed the idea of the "guided tour."

Although Cook's agency expanded and opened branch offices, including the United States, the first American travel agency was the American Express Company. American Express was also the first company to offer traveler's checks, which made it easier for travelers to Europe to obtain cash. The company's financial strength and guarantee to back the checks helped to gain acceptance of them around the world. By the turn of the century, there were several travel agencies in the U.S. and the travel industry was growing rapidly.

It was during the 20th century that the travel agent gained prominence. As the desire for travel grew, it became clear to many enterprising individuals that arranging trips could be a complex, time-consuming effort, particularly if the trip was one of long distance or duration. These travel services entrepreneurs would undertake the task of arranging for transportation and accommodations for individuals, typically charging a fee (commission) on the costs of the products and services of travel suppliers.

The system developed quickly and soon travel agencies – much like other small, storefront businesses – began to appear in cities and major towns throughout the country. As the system became more sophisticated, travel suppliers such as airlines, railroads, and cruise operators realized the need to ensure the safety of their tickets and preferred to work with travel agents they felt they could trust. This trust was generally founded on the fact that the travel agency operated out of a storefront office, was bonded, and respectable.

This system dominated the travel industry until the last two decades of the 20th century and the explosion of the technological revolution. Computers changed the travel industry. With a computer and the proper software, individuals can do just about everything a travel agent working in an office agency can do. This development has opened the travel industry to anyone who has an interest in providing travel and related services.

No longer is it necessary to maintain a storefront agency. Agents can work out of their homes, reducing their overhead and enjoying more independence. Indeed, home-based travel agencies are being established at an increasing rate while storefront agencies, especially the small ones, are closing. It should be noted that many of the storefront agencies that close are re-opened as home-based agencies.

# Different Kinds of Travel Agencies

While early travel agencies were all-purpose companies, handling all kinds of travel and working to satisfy whatever needs their clients might have, many of today's agencies specialize. The categories often overlap, but agencies can be divided into several major groups:

- **The Full Service Agency.** This agency assumes management of all the client's travel needs. Full service agencies offer tours, vacation travel for individuals and families, group travel, and business travel. Many large full service agencies are quite profitable and maintain numerous branches.

- **The Commercial Agency.** This agency concentrates its operations on companies, corporations, and business travelers. While they usually possess expertise in handling all aspects of travel for their clients, they offer few or no services to individuals and families, unless they are affiliated with a business client. Because of their focus on business clients, many of which are large companies, commercial agencies can be very successful.

- **The Group Agency.** Group agencies gear their operations to special groups and usually provide services regarding tours. Some group agencies work closely with full-service agencies, which may handle the actual bookings. In such cases, profits are split.

- **The In-house Agency**. This agency is most typically a branch office of a travel agency, but it is located within a major corporate client's facilities. The purpose of the in-house agency is to manage all of the client's travel needs.

- **The Home-based Travel Agency.** In this agency, the travel agent works out of his or her home, usually from a small office. Overhead is low, however, the quality of service can often surpass that of other agencies because the owner-entrepreneur has a personal stake in his agency's success. While some "home" travel agents manage the bookings for their clients, others work with large agencies, which may handle the actual arrangements. Profits are shared. Home-based travel agencies can be successful, not only in terms of financial gain, but also of the many advantages the travel agent enjoys.

# The Home-based Travel Agency

Home-based travel agencies can operate in different ways. Generally, a home-based agency is a business engaged in the selling of travel services from an office in one's home. Some home-based agents function much like a full-service agency, handling all aspects of a client's travel needs, but many others work out of their home as a representative of a larger agency, often called the host agency.

The arrangement works much as a partnership, except that the home-based agent retains his or her independence. The home-based agent markets his services, prospects for, and signs customers, and then the host agency provides any required tickets and makes the necessary arrangements with travel suppliers. The host agency shares the commission it earns from the travel suppliers with the home-based agent.

Because the home-based agent is in fact an independent contractor, he can decide if he wants to work with a host agency, and, if he does, which ones. There usually is some room to negotiate regarding the split in commissions, as well as how the relationship between home-based agent and host agency will operate. Some home-based agents do some of the booking of trips while others may simply act as referral agents. After signing clients these home-based agents simply send the details to the host agency. Some home-based agents specialize, perhaps focusing their business on cruises or niche tours, while some will handle just about any kind of trip.

Because home-based agents maintain a large measure of independence, they determine whether their agency will be a full-time or part-time business. They decide how many hours they will work and what type of services they will offer. Becoming a home-based agent gives you much latitude in creating your business.

## The Value of a Host Agency

The majority of home-based travel agents work with one or more host agencies. The typical host agency enjoys ARC/ IATAN status, is bonded, and trusted by airlines to ensure the security of their tickets. ARC is an acronym for Airlines Reporting Corporation; IATAN stands for the International Airlines Travel Agency Network. Travel agents need access to both if they are to provide their clients with airline tickets. Because most airlines are reluctant to work with independent home-based travel agents (although there are exceptions, for example, if the travel agent has a long-standing relationship with the airlines), most home-based agents need a host agency to ensure that they can obtain tickets. Moreover, only agencies that enjoy ARC/IATAN designation can collect commissions paid on airline tickets. The relationship benefits both sides. While the home-based travel agent needs the host agency to obtain airline tickets, most host agencies welcome the business home-based agents bring them.

Although they appreciate the commissions they share with host agencies, most home-based agents understand that they earn more profit when they can arrange travel packages themselves. Even though home-based agents must rely on a host agency for airline tickets, many cruises and tours can be arranged by independents. When home-based agents arrange for trips without a host agency, they earn all of the commissions.

Many travel suppliers, especially those that offer cruises, tours, and special vacation packages, are willing to work with independent, home-based agents in the same manner they work with ARC/IATAN agencies, provided the home-based agent provides them with a fair and consistent amount of business. In other words, the more business you provide to suppliers, the more willing they are to treat you as a major agency with the same status and commissions.

For the entrepreneur who desires to establish a travel agency, the best course is to set up his agency in his home. This gives him the greatest control of his business. If in time, after the business has grown, he decides to obtain office space, he will be doing so with the knowledge that he has already built a client base. At that time, if he wishes, he can decide to apply for ARC/IATAN appointment. (ARC/IATAN appointments will be discussed in length in Chapter 2, "Setting Up Your Home-based Travel Agency.")

Whether the owner-entrepreneur remains working from an office in his home, or establishes a larger office, he will have great flexibility in deciding how to operate his agency. Most home-based, independent travel agents build a network through which they work with resorts, cruise lines, airlines, hotels, and other travel agencies. Many develop working relationships with inside travel agents – those who work in other agencies for a salary. The independent agent brings business to the inside travel agent, who may make all of the arrangements. Fees are split. In such cases, the independent travel agent prospects for clients, while leaving the meticulous details of booking to others. Partnerships like this are usually beneficial to all parties. In many cases, they are a necessity.

You should avoid the temptation of becoming an inside agent for someone else's agency. Inside agents are usually salaried, with entry level positions receiving meager compensation. Even those inside agents who have been with a company for several years seldom command high salaries. Working as an independent for yourself is generally more rewarding in pay and satisfaction.

## Establishing Yourself as a Travel Agent

Depending upon how you wish to establish your travel agency, you may rent or buy an office or you may prefer to work out of your home. A home-based agency is ideal if you intend to limit the amount of time you spend on travel-related matters. Many individuals these days are part-time travel agents, working out of their homes. They often maintain other occupations. They set their own hours as travel agents, limit their clientele – perhaps to friends, relatives, or business associates – but are still able to enjoy the many benefits of being a travel agent.

# The Benefits of Being a Travel Agent

Few people outside of the travel and tourism industry are fully aware of the many benefits the typical travel agent enjoys. These benefits are, indeed, numerous and impressive, including:

- Since income is derived primarily from commissions, your earnings are directly related to your own efforts.

- You will enjoy the tax benefits of owning and operating a small business.

- You will travel the world over at reduced rates and use this as an opportunity to find investment opportunities in other countries.

- If you establish your own agency (which is recommended rather than working for someone else), you are your own boss.

- You can set your own hours.

- You decide where your travel agency will be located – in an office building or in your home.

- In most cases you receive money back on each vacation or business trip you take.

- When you travel, you will enjoy some of the lowest rates available – often reserved only for travel agents.

- You will enjoy upgrades to better hotel rooms and airline seats because of your status as a travel agent.

- You will enjoy travel agent discounts on tours, hotels, and even restaurants. Hotel discounts can sometimes be as much as 70%, depending upon the season and rate of occupancy.

- You will enjoy special travel agent rates on rental cars.

- You will enjoy deep discounts for vacation packages for you and your family.

- You will enjoy familiarization trips sponsored by cruise lines and resorts. These can often be had for greatly reduced rates and in some cases can be had virtually for free.

- You can decide the scope of your business. You may, for example, prefer to specialize in vacation travel, business travel, or commercial travel.

- You will enjoy reduced rates for admission to theme parts and resorts.

- You will work in a field that is exciting and satisfying.

Travel agents, unquestionably, enjoy a variety of significant benefits. The only limitations are those that the agent imposes upon himself.

# Special Training

In the past, many people who wished to enter the travel industry simply applied for a job with an established agency, entered the field at the bottom level, learned from experience, and rose through promotions. They learned by observing and working with seasoned travel agents.

Today, training programs and courses abound. Many four-year and community colleges offer complete, comprehensive programs in tourism and travel management. Many adult evening schools offer classes in local high schools. To find these offerings, simply contact colleges, adult education programs, or your local state board of education.

While most travel and tourism courses are run by competent professionals, you should make certain that the courses you intend to take will be effective and will provide you with the training you expect. Here are some points to consider:

- Is the school licensed, approved, or accredited by a state agency or bureau?

- Is the instructor knowledgeable and experienced? What is his background? Ideally, he is a travel agent who is still active in the field. Such experience can be valuable.

- What will you learn in the course? A good course will offer vital information in all areas of the travel profession, including: an overview of the industry and its methods and procedures, such as booking airlines, cruises, and tours, marketing and sales, information on geography and places of destination.

- Will you learn how to incorporate the computer in your travel agency? Computers have become essential to the travel industry and you are unlikely to achieve success unless you have a thorough understanding of how to use computers in travel management.

- Does the school or course sponsors have ties to the travel industry? Can they help you establish your business once you complete the course? What, if any, kind of support do they offer once you have finished the course?

Questions such as these can help you determine if a course or school will be helpful to you in your goal of becoming a travel agent. To be successful in the travel industry, an individual must have specialized skills and knowledge. A thorough education in travel management can be a great advantage.

Most states in the U.S. do not require any special degree or license for individuals to offer travel services. Only Florida, Rhode Island, Iowa, Illinois, Ohio, Washington, California, Oregon, and Hawaii require travel agents to register or obtain state certification. Other states and local jurisdictions may have regulations regarding registration and you should check with local and state authorities before you offer services. Even for those places that do require registration, in most cases this is just a formality and the filing of forms.

# Reasons for Establishing a Home-based Travel Agency

Every year ambitious, industrious individuals enter the travel and tourism field with lofty goals of building their own business and getting rich. Most fail miserably. While some, clearly, are not cut out to run a business, most entered the field with the wrong assumptions and goals.

This does not mean that there are individuals who establish successful home-based agencies, nor does it mean that an individual can't make an excellent salary selling travel services from his or her home. Many do. But successful individuals invariably entered the field for the right reasons, including:

- They love to travel.

- They possess an entrepreneurial spirit and desire to build and operate their own business.

- They enjoy working with people.

- They understand that hard work is the only true path to success.

- They are willing to locate customers and sell travel services.

- They utilize their travel agent advantages to seek out investment opportunities in other parts of the world.

Establishing a home-based travel agency is not a quick way to riches. Like most businesses it takes time to nurture and grow. You can expect problems to arise and hard decisions will need to be made.

The positives far outweigh the negatives, however. Successful travel agents can earn excellent money, but even more importantly, they reap the benefits of the profession. Those with an entrepreneurial spirit can roam the world at little cost looking for investment opportunities as well as for pleasure. For such individuals, becoming a travel agent is a means to an end.

# Setting Up Your Home-based Travel Agency

Establishing your travel agency in your home will bestow many advantages. Because your workplace is your home, you will not incur commuting costs, nor will you have to support the overhead of renting or buying office space. You will decide when you want to work and how long you work. Perhaps most importantly, your success will be determined directly through your own efforts.

People start home businesses with various goals. Some intend to build the business and make it their sole occupation. Others are satisfied with the home business providing supplemental income. These people keep their day jobs and don't plan to run their home business full-time. (This often changes, however, when the home business becomes more lucrative than the day job.) Still others view a home business as a hobby. They operate the business because they enjoy what they are doing.

Before you establish your home-based travel agency, you need to consider the viability of starting an agency. Since most new businesses fail within the first three years, you need to assess your situation and weigh the chances that you will be successful. You should consider the following:

- Will there be a market for your travel services in the area you intend to establish your agency? What is your competition? What edge, or plan, do you have to beat the competition? Perhaps your closest competition will be a full-service agency, and you might be able to offer specialized tours for specific groups.

- Do you have the room to establish an agency in your home? If not, can you afford to rent or purchase office space?

- Are you an entrepreneur? Do you have the nature to own and operate a business? Creating and running a business requires commitment, hard work, and perseverance. This is true even of small home-based businesses.

- Do you have the necessary financial reserves to sustain you and your family until your business becomes profitable? Most new businesses do not show a profit until the third year of operation. If you lack the funds, do you have access to funds, perhaps through friends or relatives? It is not a good idea to take a second mortgage on your house to finance your new business. Banks and other lending institutions are generally reluctant to loan money to people who wish to start a home business, unless they are given strong reasons why the business is likely to succeed.

An option to establishing a new business is to purchase an existing one or buy a franchise. In either case, you will require investment money. Note: Buying an existing travel agency or a franchise can be a complicated procedure and you should consult your attorney and accountant before moving ahead.

After assessing your situation and deciding that you do indeed wish to start a travel agency, you need to consider what you would like your business to become. If your objective is to build a full-time business, your goals, especially those affecting your operations over the long-term, will be different than if you intend your business to remain a part-time activity. Indeed, formulating and setting goals is a critical step in the founding of any business.

Effective goal-setting requires that you consider all aspects of your business. You should set both short- and long-term goals. View your goals as the beacons from lighthouses that guide you forward across the business sea. They help you to stay the course, and give you a feeling of accomplishment once they are attained. Without goals, you risk floating adrift. Rather than moving forward, you may meander or stall; you won't be zeroed in on success and are unlikely to achieve it.

When formulating goals, you must be realistic. Unrealistic goals are unattainable and you will only be setting yourself up for failure. The best goals are those that require you to work hard but which are, in the end, achievable. Such goals will pull you forward toward success.

When you set goals for your travel agency, consider the following:

- What kind of agency do you wish to establish? Is it your hope to begin a part-time operation and eventually build it to a full-time occupation? Do you want it simply as a supplemental income? Do you wish to become a travel agent so that you can benefit from the travel discounts agents typically enjoy. The type of agency you wish to establish will impact upon the decisions you will need to make.

- What type of travel services do you wish to offer? While full-service agencies work with individuals and business clients, many travel agents specialize.

You may, for example, specialize in providing cruises, island vacations, or tour packages for families. You may concentrate your efforts on hideaway vacation spots, or European getaways aimed at niche markets. Or, you may decide that you wish to focus on corporate clients and business travel.

- Do you intend to work with a host agency? Or will you apply for ARC/IATAN designation?

- How much monthly income will you need from your agency? If you plan to work at another job and use the profits from your travel agency as a supplement to your income, your income goals will be quite different than if you plan to work as a travel agent full-time. You should project your anticipated income for each of the first three years.

- You must anticipate the hiring of staff, particularly if you intend to build your business. If you need to hire staff, will you still be able to work from your home, or will you need to rent office space? Even though you may not need to address such concerns during your first year, considering them in the early going helps to reduce the chances for unwelcomed surprises.

# Putting the Pieces in Place

There is much to do *before* starting your travel agency. Only after completing thorough research and evaluation of market conditions, your resources, and competition can you make a reasonable prediction of the chances of success for your venture.

One of the first steps is to become familiar with the travel industry. Reading this book is a good start, but you should consult several other sources as well. Learn as much as you can. Once you start your business, experience will add to your knowledge and expertise.

Before committing yourself to any start-up operations, you must assess the advantages of a home-based travel agency as opposed to a storefront office. For most people, in the current travel environment, a home-based agency is the more practical choice. When working out of your home, your overhead costs are greatly reduced and you have more time to build your client base. Moreover, you will not be burdened with the added responsibilities of maintaining a big office, which will allow you to devote more of your energy to selling travel services. Remember, a home-based operation can always be expanded based upon its sales and profitability.

You must also decide what form your business will take. You may prefer to run your business as a sole proprietorship, partnership, or a corporation. Each has advantages and disadvantages and you should evaluate each in terms of what one will best satisfy your needs and goals. In a sole proprietorship, you maintain complete control of your business. In a partnership, you share the control and responsibility for your travel agency with one or more other individuals. Their work and expertise can relieve you of many burdens, not the least of which is a sharing of the start-up costs. A corporation gives you instant credibility, shields your personal assets from any debts the company incurs, and can bring more tax advantages but there is more paperwork and fees. Incorporating adds to your start-up costs but can save you money later.

Following are the major advantages and disadvantages of the three main business structures:

- **Sole proprietorship:** The simplest legal structure in which you are owner and manager of your business. You make all the decisions and control all the profits. However, because you personally own the business, your personal assets are potentially at risk should the business fail. Since the laws of states vary somewhat regarding sole proprietorships, consult your attorney about the types of personal property that might be considered separate from your business and therefore shielded.

- **Partnership:** In this business structure, two or more people share the ownership of a business. While each individual brings his expertise to the new company, and potentially financial backing, partners are legally liable for each other's actions. Debts are likewise shared, regardless of who incurred them in the name of the business. Furthermore, if partners do not have equal shares, the partner who controls the most may assume he has the right to make all final decisions. When working smoothly, partnerships can build on the resources and abilities of the partners; unfortunately, when they don't, they can result in a failing business and legal mess.

- **Corporation:** The major advantage of creating a corporation is that the corporation, by law, is considered to be a separate entity and possesses the legal rights of an individual. Corporations are regulated far more tightly than partnerships and sole proprietorships, and you should consult with an attorney before attempting to form one. If you intend to keep your business small, focusing on special interest groups, a corporation may not be worth the additional required paperwork and start-up costs.

Whether you decide to structure your travel agency as a sole proprietorship, partnership, or corporation, before actually starting, you must research your market. Who will your customers be? Will you be located in area where a large pool of potential travelers exists? Locating your home-based agency in a small remote mountain town might be picturesque, but it is unlikely to be the home of many travelers. A good-sized city or affluent suburban area would be a better choice, however, there is also likely to be more competition here.

Along with researching your market you must evaluate your competition fully. If your area of business already has several established travel agencies, it will be difficult for you to build a client base unless you offer truly exceptional packages. Even then you will likely need to lure clients from other agencies. The ideal location is an area where people are relatively affluent, travel regularly, and is not saturated with competing agencies.

Before opening your business, you must estimate your start-up costs. This will help to ensure that you have adequate financial reserves to get your travel agency started.

Following is a list of the major start-up costs you must con sider:

- Rent for office space or costs for purchase. (A home office will greatly reduce or eliminate these expenses.)

- Legal and other fees.

- Accounting fees.

- Furniture (desks, chairs, tables, filing cabinets, shelves, fixtures, etc.)

- Equipment (computer, printer, telephone, answering machine, copier), including any costs for installation.

- Advertising and promotions.

- Office supplies (paper, envelopes, letterheads, etc.)

- Insurance and any bonds that might need to be posted.

- Subscriptions to manuals, travel journals, etc.

- Salaries for staff (if any).

- Costs for utilities, although if your agency is to be located in your home, you will not be paying directly for utilities. You may be able to deduct a portion of your utilities at tax time because of your business. Check with your accountant.

After considering the above and arriving at an estimated total, you should add another 10% for unexpected costs. Remember, the list above includes the common costs of starting a travel agency. Depending upon your situation, there might be others and you must plan for them.

After assessing your potential costs, you must evaluate your finances and determine if you have enough funding to start and maintain your new business. A home-based travel agency requires much less financial investment than an agency that needs to rent or purchase office space. Because of the low costs associated with a home-based travel agency, most entrepreneurs usually finance the start-up costs themselves.

A home-based agency requires little more than a desk, computer table, computer, printer, on-line connection, copier, telephone, message recorder, and fax machine. The room can be a small extra bedroom, or you might even use your dining room table. Keep in mind, though, that if you intend to meet with clients in your home, a separate room for an office will make a better impression. Some travel agents who work out of their home meet with client's in the client's home. This serves two functions: It eliminates the need for a home office in a separate room, and is often more convenient to the client who does not have to travel to meet with you. Many clients appreciate such consideration.

Although ample sources of funding exist to establish business enterprises, you will likely need to search out the best sources for your plans. Personal savings, friends, relatives, banks, and credit unions are some of the best sources. Whenever you approach anyone regarding investment in your new travel agency, you need to present them with a well-conceived business plan. This is particularly true of financial institutions who will assess what they feel is your overall chance for success through your business plan that should include your goals and how you expect to reach them.

## Preparing a Business Plan

A good business plan is your plan for success. While business plans vary in form and length – obviously your home-based travel agency's plan will be different than the business plan for a fledgling high-tech company – all sound business plans share much in common. At their minimal they provide information about a business's general operations, products and/or services, ownership, management, general costs, and sources of funding.

A thorough business plan is essential in the securing of funding to back your travel agency. Banks and other financial institutions, as well as individuals who are considering investing in your idea, are more likely to support you if they see that you have a plan that gives you a chance to become profitable. A comprehensive business plan shows others that you are serious about your proposed travel agency, and that you have given the matter much thought.

A quality business plan is written in clear, straightforward language, and is based on facts. Projections should be realistic and exaggerations avoided. You should provide explanations and specific data as much as possible. Following is a structure you might consider using for your travel agency:

- **Goals and Objectives.** Your goals and objectives describe what your travel agency will do and what you hope to achieve.

- **General Operations.** You should describe how your business will be run. Will you operate as a sole proprietorship, partnership, or corporation?

Will you operate from a home office or rent or purchase office space? Will you have any employees? If yes, how many? Will you work with a host agency?

- **Services.** Your business plan should include a complete description of what services you will offer. Will you specialize on certain types of travel? For instance, tours? Or will you handle all types of travel? Offer details how you will satisfy the needs of your clients.

- **Potential Market.** Your potential market should be fully delineated in your business plan. Who, exactly, are you targeting as clients? The general traveler? Families? Business travelers? Special groups? Provide information how you intend to reach these people, and why they would buy travel services from you.

- **Your Competition.** A solid business plan includes specific details about the competition. Who they are and what advantages, if any, they might have should be addressed. You should also explain how you intend to overcome your competition. Your major competition might, for example, focus their energies on business travelers, vacations, and cruises. This might leave you with an opportunity to exploit specialty tours for interested groups.

- **Management.** Your business plan should include detailed information about how your company will be run. Will you manage it? Will your hire others? If your company is to be a partnership, which partner will be responsible for which duties? Will any partner have the deciding voice? Also important here is your experience and the experiences of anyone you might have working for you. If, for example, you have worked in the travel and tourism industry for several years, you would be bringing this wealth of experience to your business.

- **Technology.** You should include the types and level of technology your travel agency will utilize. Obviously, computers are crucial to the travel agent for they are vital for bookings, confirmations, and reference.

- **Finances.** Your business plan should detail at least three years of your anticipated expenses and income. All potential costs should be listed and realistic projections for income should be provided.

- **Financial Resources.** This section of your business plan should include all potential sources of income that will sustain your travel agency through the first few years of business. You should include any personal resources you have committed – this can often convince other sources of your sincerity and belief in your travel agency – as well as other potential sources.

- **Relationships.** You should describe and explain any special relationships you might have, or intend to, develop with host agencies or travel service suppliers. Small companies can often carve out profitable niches by working with others.

Your business plan need not be overly long. It does need to be clear, specific, and factual. Business plans that are accurate and detailed provide the business owner with valuable insight as to his overall operation, and also impress others with the entrepreneur's thoroughness in preparation for his business venture. A solid plan also is more likely to favorably impress potential sources of investment than a plan that is too brief, overloaded with lofty claims for success, or exaggerates facts.

# The Final Steps

Even after you have researched your market, decided on where your travel agency will be located, prepared a business plan, and arranged for financing, there is still more you

must do before you open for business. Consider the follow
ing:

- Select a name for your agency. You might use
  your name, as in John Doe Travel Agency, or you
  might conceive a name: Speedy Travel.

- Decide whether to team up with host agencies,
  particularly if you will require their help in
  obtaining tickets or securing travel arrangements.

- Complete any registrations, forms for certification,
  or licenses with your state or local government.
  Your attorney can help you with this.

- Set up your travel agency as a sole proprietorship,
  partnership, or corporation. Again, your attorney
  can handle the details.

- Consult with your accountant and acquire any
  federal identification numbers you might need.

- If you are leasing or buying office space, make
  the final transactions. Be sure to have your
  attorney review all contracts.

- Open a bank account in your business's name.

- Place any final orders for furniture, equipment,
  etc.

- Arrange furniture and equipment in your office.

- Design a letterhead, order stationery, envelopes, and other office supplies.

- Obtain bonding, if necessary.

- Obtain insurance. Checking with your agent will help to ensure that you obtain the proper coverage, including liability.

- If you wish to obtain ARC/IATAN designation, apply now. (See the next section for details.)

- Begin advertising. Signs, advertisements in local newspapers, a listing (and ad) in the Yellow Pages, and perhaps local mailings can inform the community that you are opening a travel agency. Be sure to list the travel services you are offering in your advertising.

- Contact travel suppliers such as cruise lines, tour operators, and vacation packagers that you are a new agency. Request any brochures, pamphlets, and any other information they can provide.

- Hire staff, if any.

- Place subscriptions to travels journals, manuals, and other publications that will enable you to keep abreast of travel trends.

- Set up computers and put in place software for your business operations.

You are now ready for the final step: Begin your business and welcome clients.

# Should You Apply for ARC/IATAN Appointments

The Airlines Reporting Corporation (ARC) and the International Airlines Travel Agency Network (IATAN) are essential for coordinating airline ticket sales, refunds, exchanges, and payment of commissions. ARC and IATAN are similar in purpose and function, but there are some differences. ARC will be examined first.

ARC enables travel agents to sell airline tickets efficiently. Although travel agents are not required to be appointed by ARC to sell airline tickets, earn commissions, or obtain reduced rates for their clients, it is difficult for them to compete with agents that have obtained the appointment.

Quite simply, airlines prefer to deal with agents who have obtained ARC appointment because in their eyes such agents are more trustworthy. An independent travel agent can contact the various airlines and attempt to arrange an agreement in which he would sell airline tickets on commission, however, he would need to make arrangements with all of the major airlines and most of the large regional ones. This process borders on the impossible, especially given the reluctance of airlines to bargain with non-ARC agencies. There is simply too much paperwork and too much risk.

The major advantage of obtaining an ARC appointment is that the travel agent can use ARC standard ticket stock for issuing tickets for any travel supplier that belongs to ARC. This includes more than 100 domestic and international carriers.

To obtain an ARC appointment you must obtain and maintain a bond or irrevocable letter of credit in the amount of $20,000. This bond assures ARC of your trustworthiness as an ARC appointed travel agent. Essentially, it screens out those shoestring operations that might become bankrupt and default on their ARC obligations.

For additional information on ARC, contact:

> Airlines Reporting Corporation (ARC)
> 1530 Wilson Blvd., Suite 800
> Arlington, VA 22209-2448
> Tel: 703-816-8000
> Fax: 703-816-8104

If you choose not to obtain an ARC appointment, it is likely that you will need to establish a relationship with a host agency (or agencies) that do enjoy ARC designation. It is through your host agency that you can obtain airline tickets for your client, splitting commissions with the host agency. For many home-based agents, working with a host agency is an agreeable option.

IATAN functions similarly to ARC and unless you wish to issue airline tickets for airlines that do not participate in ARC, it is probable that you do not need an IATAN appointment. The requirements of IATAN appointment are similar (though not exact) to ARC. For more information, contact:

> International Airlines Travel Agent Network
> (IATAN)
> P.O. Box 2988
> Plattsburgh, NY 12901-0269
> Tel: 516-747-4716

# Avoiding the Traps That Lie in Wait of New Businesses

More businesses fail each year in the U.S. than succeed. Indeed, in some business sectors, the failure rate during the first five years is close to 80%. While the combination of factors that affect the failure or success of every business is unique to that business, some factors regularly conspire to undermine even companies founded in expanding fields. Being aware of such factors can help you to avoid the traps that ensure and ruin new companies. The following traps regularly cause business failures:

- Inadequate customer base.

- Inadequate control of costs.

- Inadequate collection of payments.

- Underpricing of services or products.

- Poor marketing.

- Weak customer relationships.

- Little return business.

- Failure to maintain positive relations with suppliers.

- Mismanagement.

- Inexperience.

- Insufficient capital.

- Hiring of inexperienced or unqualified staff.

- Inadequate training of staff.

- Poor location.

- Inadequate use of technology.

- Inability to promote and sell services or products due to lack of initiative or understanding of service/product.

- Inability of management to make decisions.

- Poor personnel relations, resulting in loss of quality staff.

- Failure to understand and react positively to market trends.

- Inability to identify and develop a competitive edge.

- Poor bookkeeping.

- Failure to assess expenses and income effectively, leading to miscalculation of budgets.

- Unwillingness to consult professional advice (lawyers, accountants, etc.) when necessary.

- Negligence in regard to completing proper registrations, licenses, and certifications when applicable.

- Ignoring the use of tax reduction to increase profitability.

- Failure to invest profits, which could lead to an increase in income and earnings.

While the above apply to virtually any business, the following traps apply specifically to entrepreneurs who establish a home-based enterprise. If you wish to achieve success with your home-based travel agency, you would do well to adhere to the following:

- Set up your office in a separate room or at least away from the main traffic of your home. This will help to ensure that you can maintain privacy when working.

- Make a schedule of your working hours. If your home-based agency is part-time, you might set aside the hours of six to nine in the evening and ten to five on Saturdays. During these times, family members should realize that you are not to be disturbed. Treat your office hours as if you were away on business.

- Close your office door to avoid interruptions.

- Maintain a separate computer system, phone, fax machine and answering machine in your office.

- If necessary, arrange for child care for young children when you are working. You cannot expect to work efficiently if you have to take care of children.

- Include your spouse and older children in the business. They can easily help you with the many tasks you will need to do.

There are many advantages to operating your travel agency out of your home. You must, however, remember that it is a business and must be treated as a business.

# Making Your Home Office Efficient

Because the mere location of a home office gives rise to numerous temptations you would not encounter in a storefront office – frequent trips to the refrigerator, for example, or walking the dog because you want a change of scenery – you need to make a strong effort for efficiency. Moreso than storefront offices, it is easy for the routines of a home office to slip into complacency, which in time may threaten the business's success. The following suggestions can help you to keep your home-based travel agency working at top efficiency:

- Set and strive for clear goals.

- Set priorities. Handle important tasks first and non-essential tasks later.

- Break large tasks into workable parts. Manage the tasks in a logical order.

- Organize tasks into groups. For example, set aside a time of the day when you return phone, another part of the day for working on your computer, and another time for reviewing data about travel sites.

- Remain flexible and revise your schedule for efficiency. If your computer goes down, make phone calls to clients, balance your books, or review information from brochures. Fill your time with productive minutes.

- Assess your operations monthly. Keep track of your progress on your goals. As you reach goals, set new ones.

Unquestionably, there is much to establishing a home-based travel agency. There is even more to do should you decide to open a storefront agency. The entrepreneur who considers the various aspects of starting a travel agency – business structure, market, competition, and financial resources – and evaluates the many factors honestly and thoroughly, measuring them in the light of potential profitability is far more likely to be successful than the entrepreneur who begins his business with little prior research or thought. While it is true that new businesses fail at a higher rate than those that succeed, it is also true that the owners of successful businesses take the proper steps to ensure their success. By taking those same steps you will increase the chances of your travel agency's success.

# Marketing Your Travel Services

While an effective marketing program will not propel an otherwise poorly run business to profitability, without a sound marketing program even an efficiently operated company will not realize its greatest potential earnings. Making a profit in business comes down to one factor: effective marketing.

Marketing covers a broad range of activities and procedures. At its most basic, the purpose of a marketing program is to make people aware of your business and attract potential buyers of the services you offer. Marketing includes planning, advertising, research, image, packaging, promotions – and any other activity that informs people of your travel agency and the services it offers. Many small and particularly home-based businesses do not spend enough time on marketing. When you consider that most large companies employ marketing departments, whose purpose is to concentrate entirely on marketing, you will begin to realize the importance of a marketing program. If you do not make the public aware of your business, it is improbable that you will have much business.

# What Marketing Entails

Marketing is a tough job because there are always so many things to do. Assuming that you will not be hiring a marketing person for your travel agency, the responsibility for your agency's marketing program will fall to you. Following are just some of the duties you will assume:

- Identify potential clients for your travel services.

- Identify the travel needs of potential clients. Perhaps you are located in a suburban area and most of your clients will be families seeking vacation arrangements.

- Identify and study your competition. Try to find niche markets that your competitors may have missed or choose to ignore. These can often be profitable.

- Develop a marketing program that includes advertising in any or all of the following: the

Yellow Pages, local newspapers, magazines, direct mail, local radio, and perhaps even TV spots.

- Build contacts with local reporters, TV and radio personalities, and other media outlets. Media contacts can often lead to exceptional opportunities. Imagine a local reporter you know who considers doing a human interest story on home businesses, and he picks yours. Such free publicity is extremely valuable.

- Network with local and regional business leaders. This is a fine way to obtain corporate clients.

- Join local community groups, particularly the Chamber of Commerce and charity groups, as a way of expanding your contacts and making others aware of your agency.

- Track the travel market and look for new trends on which you might be able to capitalize.

- Make available various brochures, pamphlets, flyers, and announcements to keep the public aware of your travel agency.

- Maintain contact with clients, especially corporate travelers, to make sure that they are satisfied with your services. It also helps to acknowledge events such as birthdays, promotions, and special company-sponsored activities. Sending a note or card will impress your client with your thoughtfulness and remind him of your services.

- Research travel destinations to enhance personal knowledge of the places clients might wish to visit.

Without question, marketing should be one of your most important tasks. In most cases, businesses that market their services and products effectively and consistently earn greater profits than those who fail to give marketing the time and consideration it demands.

# Finding Clients for Your Travel Services

Selling is the name of the game. If you do not sell your travel services, you will not attain profitability. Next to marketing, selling will likely be your most important activity. Marketing brings potential clients to your agency; selling results in their buying your services.

Selling can arise from various situations. An individual may call and ask you to arrange a trip to the West Coast. He knows where he wishes to go, when he wants to leave and return, and where he wants to stay upon arrival. He agrees to your price and you have made an easy sale. Sometimes people will contact you after seeing an advertisement or reading one of your brochures. You will provide them with information, but they do not purchase your services at that time. Perhaps they are not certain about the trip, or they may decide to shop around for better deals. In this case, you should call back in a few days and discuss the benefits of your services with the individual. Maybe you can suggest alternative destinations. Never forget – persistence leads to sales.

Potential clients, called prospects, are all around you. You already know many of them. Here are just some:

- Relatives.

- Friends.

- Neighbors.

- Colleagues of your full-time job.

- Community groups to which you belong.

- Church groups of which you are a member.

- Other business people in your area – your barber, beautician, owner of your local deli, your lawn service representative, dog groomer, office supply store, etc.

- Members of the general public.

Acquaintances will be your greatest source of clients in the early days of your agency. Most people prefer to make their travel plans with a person they know and trust. Why shouldn't that be you rather than someone else? Of course, they won't book their plans through you if they don't know about your travel agency.

Once you have established your agency, you must inform others about it. While advertising will help to inform the general public, you should contact friends, associates, and acquaintances in person. Call or meet with them, explain your services, and let them know you will be happy to help them arrange their next vacation or travel plans. Provide potential clients with brochures that explain your services and which include your phone and fax number. Ask those with whom you speak to refer others to your travel agency. Such efforts help you to expand your circle of contacts.

As you begin to create a customer base, you must maintain accurate records. Keep a Rolodex or thorough list of all your clients, as well as those individuals you have contacted even if they have not booked services with you. Marketing lists can help you to keep in touch with potential clients and keep them aware of your agency.

Always carry your business card with you and be ready to hand it out. Most potential clients when planning a trip will be happy to discuss it with you. After all, they know you and trust you. Many would find it more assuring to have you arrange their trip rather than a stranger. Of course, these feelings are predicated on the fact that you have created a solid business image and offer valuable travel services at a fair price. Friends, relatives, neighbors, and associates are also likely to recommend your service to others, especially if they are pleased with the arrangements you made on their behalf. Such word-of-mouth referrals can turn in to valuable business.

While you should certainly seek clients among those you know, you must also try to find clients among the general population and especially the business community. Business travelers and corporate clients in particular can be a superior source of income. Although most major companies will buy their travel services from large agencies, or they might even have in-house agents serve their needs, there are plenty of small and mid-sized firms that require travel from time to time. Securing such companies as clients can lead to regular sales. Moreover, once you have developed a working relationship with them and they are satisfied with your service, they will come to you first for their travel needs. Repeat business is a crucial factor in any company's bottom line.

You will probably have to make the first contact with potential business clients. A good method is to send a promotional package that includes the various travel services you provide. You should follow this up with a personal note and phone call in which you request a meeting so that you can provide details of your travel service. Be polite, considerate, but persistent.

When you meet, be sure to point out that you can handle all of the company's travel needs. During your discussion, find out what, precisely, their needs for traveling are and explain how you can manage the arrangements. Emphasize that all they need to do is call you, and you will handle all the details. Further, emphasize the benefits using your service will bring to the client. Note that your service is personal, thorough, and fast. You might also, for example, accept a slightly lower fee to ensure that you gain and retain a client's business, especially if the client travels regularly. The lower fees will be more than offset by steady business.

Whenever you meet with business clients, be sure to provide them with plenty of information byway of maps of the area they will be visiting, special tips for lodging, and any other information they will find useful. Identify the most direct routes for them and the best places to stay that are within their budgets. Always be ready to assist your clients should a flight be canceled or if they have to revise their plans during their trip.

You should follow much the same procedure with other clients. Be available for them to meet with you, determine their travel needs, and help them to plan a trip that will satisfy their goals. Always be prepared to provide information about their destination, how they will get there, and what they might expect. Providing information enhances your image in the eyes of your clients, but it also enables your clients to consider options for their trip. They will appreciate the extra "touch" you offer as opposed to other agencies that might simply want to book a trip as quickly as they can, paying little attention to the client's overall concerns.

# Reaching out to the Public

For most travel agencies, the general public is a huge market that can provide a significant amount of business. The best way to reach this market is through advertising. There are several approaches you can take:

- Display advertisements in the Yellow Pages.

- Advertisements in local newspapers.

- Advertisements in local or regional magazines.

- Fliers, posted on bulletin boards throughout your town in supermarkets and department stores.

- Direct mail.

- Billboard displays.

- Radio commercials.

- Local TV commercials.

Unless you have experience in advertising, it is advisable that you enlist the services of an advertising agency to handle your advertising program. Advertising is expensive and to be cost effective your ads must draw in clients that purchase your services. Advertising that does not attract customers is simply lost money.

You cannot, therefore, afford to mount an amateur ad campaign. While an ad in the Yellow Pages won't bankrupt a company, substantial direct mailings, spots on radio and especially TV can be very costly and can easily wreck a new company if they fail to bring in business.

Seeking the services of a professional advertising agency can be money well spent. Before you sign on, however, consult several agencies and review their work. Pay close attention to those who represent service businesses similar to yours – fellow travel agents, accountants, dentists, financial advisers – and note examples of successful advertising programs they created which you find appealing. Discuss with the company's ad director what types of advertising he recommends for you and how he would develop the program. Don't be shy when asking questions. Remember, advertising is expensive – even moreso when you fail to achieve the results you expect.

While advertising programs vary somewhat, depending upon the products or services they promote, every good advertisement includes the following elements:

- Attracts attention.

- Builds confidence.

- Arouses interest.

- Creates desire.

- Calls for action.

Because the average consumer is bombarded by thousands of advertisements each day, most screen out all except the most important ones. If your ad does not immediately seize your potential client's attention, he will probably not pay any heed to its message. After gaining attention, the ad must build in the prospect a sense of confidence that your agency can efficiently provide travel services. From there it must arouse the prospect's interest, which will help to ensure that he continues to pay attention to the advertisement. The ad must also create desire in the prospect, and make him want to use your travel services. Finally, a call for action – a powerful encouragement to motivate the potential client to take the steps to contact your agency now – is essential. Every ad should always include contact information.

The above advertising elements are a result of a variety of techniques such as headlines, colors, contrasts, photographs, illustrations, live action, catchy dialogue, smooth text, and informative details. Your ad writers can help you to select the type of advertisements that will help you to realize your goals.

Along with general advertising informing the public of your agency and the services you provide, you might also advertise special travel packages. Perhaps you have managed to put together a unique tour of Europe's hidden wonders, or you are offering winter weekends in the Caribbean. These and similar events might benefit from a special promotion. Never underestimate the power of effective advertising. It is your primary means of informing potential clients of your services.

Together with the various forms of advertising, an excellent method of informing the public about your travel services is to simply go calling on potential clients. Visit local businesses and organizations, ask to see the manager or owner, and introduce yourself. Be careful not to stay too long – that will make a bad impression on busy people – but do provide a brief overview of your travel services. Be friendly, concise, and be sure to leave a brochure and your business card. The meeting may last no more than a few minutes, but you will have made contact and have opened the door for potential business. Even if they don't need your services now, when they do have to make travel plans, they are more likely to think of you and the assistance you can provide.

# Creating Effective Advertising

Think of the many different kinds of advertisements you saw or heard today. No doubt you cannot even remember them all. Because consumers witness so many ads in one day, advertisers are constantly trying to create catchy, unusual, or arresting slogans, pictures, and actions. In creating advertisements for your travel agency, the following suggestions might prove helpful:

- Content is often more important than how your ad structured. Always offer clear details of the services you are selling.

- Good ideas are easier to sell than poor ones. Always try to highlight the best travel packages and services you offer.

- Stress the benefits your potential clients can expect to receive by purchasing services from your travel agency.

- Capture attention and sustain interest in your ad by providing valuable information in a clear manner. Freshness is critical.

- Target your advertisements to specific audiences. Ads selling vacation packages for families are not appropriate for a business market.

- Be honest. Avoid promises you may not be able to keep.

- Develop positive, upbeat ads. Avoid the negative.

- Use concise, simple language.

- Use situations and actions to which your target audience can relate.

# The Payoff of Networking

Successful entrepreneurs are always on the lookout for new clients. While servicing old customers efficiently maintains your customer base, adding new ones builds your business. One of the best, yet often overlooked, methods for finding new clients is networking.

Every community has numerous groups that are ideal for networking. Civic clubs, the local Chamber of Commerce and other business associations, the library steering committee, the PTA, little league, a local environmental organization – all of these have members who could be potential clients. You should join groups that will help you to expand your base of potential clients. Avoid simply joining the group, leaving your business card and then not attend meetings or offer little enthusiasm for the group's objectives. Genuine interest on your part will lead to new clients. Most people prefer to make their travel plans through someone they know and trust.

An effective method of finding local groups and organizations is to scan your local paper under the "Announcements" section. Most papers list the meeting times of community groups. Attend meetings, introduce yourself, and always have your business card and some brochures available. While you should not try to sell your services at the meeting, simply letting others know of what you do will bring you business.

Another method that pays off handsomely in networking is to obtain local directories. Often various business groups or realtors groups will maintain directories that they make available to other companies and organizations. Sometimes the directories are free, but most often they have a nominal fee. The payment will be a small investment for the potential clients to which you will gain access. You may also obtain directories at your local library for free. Check with your reference librarian.

Your library can be a fine source of free information. You will be able to find articles about local companies, particularly new ones being established, as well as the people managing them. New companies are likely to need travel arrangements at some time and it is unlikely that they will have contacts with travel agencies in the area. Always look for information that indicates someone might be interested in your travel services.

Marketing is crucial to the success of your travel agency. It is through marketing that you inform people of your services. Without effective marketing, even agencies with the best of services will have trouble finding clients.

# The Image of Your Travel Agency

Your travel agency will be far more successful if you develop an *image* that helps to attract potential clients. Image is a broad term that can mean different things to people. For the travel agent, or any business for that matter, it encompasses what potential clients/customers consider the services and/or products of the business to be. An image that brings to mind a professional agency that can satisfy the needs of the client efficiently is more likely to attract clients than an image that portrays the agency as a small, home-office affair. The image your agency projects elicits immediate feelings and opinions about your operations. Should your image project a negative impression, you will, unquestionably, suffer the loss of business.

Your travel agency's image arises from several factors, including:

- Visual impression.

- Verbal impression.

- Emotional impression.

The *visual impression* you and your agency make on potential clients is a result of what your client sees. A travel agent who is well groomed and dressed professionally – nice shirt, slacks, carrying a briefcase – makes a different visual impression than one who greets clients in ragged jeans, a polo shirt, and carries a frayed, worn folder. Similarly, meeting with clients at your kitchen table rather than a professional-looking home office will likely result in a negative impression. While you need not be as handsome or beautiful as a movie star, keep in mind that a smile, clean teeth, clean, attractively groomed hair, and a relaxed, friendly body language will help make people comfortable and make your sales easier.

The *verbal impression* you create is no less important. The way you speak – your vocabulary, tone, and your delivery – is used by people to determine whether they like you or not. If they do, selling travel services becomes easier.

The *emotional impression* you inspire in others will help them to decide if they trust you. If you project an image that you are calm, secure in your expertise, and willing to satisfy their travel needs, potential clients will feel comfortable dealing with you.

A positive image will help your potential clients to form a positive impression of you. They will identify you as being a person who is capable of assisting them with their travel needs. Since they perceive that you are able to help them, they will be more willing to listen to what you have to say. This is the beginning of a sale.

# Creating a Positive Image for Yourself and Your Agency

The image you create should reflect your market groups. Your first question, therefore, in developing an image is to ask yourself who your potential customers will be. Will you market your services primarily at business travelers? Will you aim your services at vacationers? Or will you specialize and offer travel packages for specific groups? Whichever market, or markets, you aim for, your image should match their expectations. If you are marketing your services to corporate executives, your attire and delivery should be on a professional level and on a par with your clients. A suit and leather briefcase are necessary. On the other hand, if you are marketing your services to families headed for vacations, you might dress more casually, perhaps slacks and a nice shirt, although your delivery should still be professional.

Always remember the old saying: "First impressions are lasting." If the image you project to potential clients is negative, it will be difficult, if not impossible, for you to change their impression. Under such circumstances, it will be equally difficult to sell them your travel services. For most clients, your first meeting will establish your image. That first meeting will also go a long way to determining sales.

# Elements of an Effective Image

Your image should communicate who you are and what you can offer to your potential clients. Moreover, everything about you and your agency should work together to advance a positive impression in the minds of your clients. The following elements can help you to build a clear and positive image for your travel agency:

- Dress and act the part of a successful travel agent. In particular, dress and act appropriately for each market segment. A caution here: Be genuine in your clothing and actions. Most people can swiftly sense phoniness and will then be leery of dealing with you. Don't try to be something you are not.

- Dress in a manner so that your client can identify with you and feel comfortable with you. Dress fashionably, avoid fads, and select clothing that accents your professionalism.

- Arrange your home office so that it is functional, professional, and efficient.

- Use business stationery for communications. Be liberal with your business cards, pamphlets, and brochures. All should be of professional caliber.

- Obtain a phone line for your business. Your voice mail greeting should identify your business, thank callers for calling, and invite them to leave a message. Make it a point to return calls.

- Always project a professional attitude. When you act professionally, potential clients will think of you as a professional and will be more willing to allow you to help them arrange their travel needs.

Potential clients will often decide whether to buy your travel services because of your image. If the image you project gives them a feeling that you are professional, trustworthy, and that you can satisfy their travel needs, they will feel comfortable dealing with you. It will not matter if you are working out of an office in your home or if your office is in a modern business complex. They will enlist your services because the image they have formed of you gives them confidence that you can meet their travel needs.

Without question, image is a crucial component of promotion, which is the foundation of your marketing program. Together, marketing and promotion are the avenues through which you inform potential clients of your services and encourage them to buy. You must make marketing and promotion a vital element of your business operations. Your overall success will be a direct result of your efforts at informing potential clients of the services you provide.

# Managing Your Travel Agency

The establishment of a new business is an exciting and challenging event, one in which the entrepreneur looks forward to the building of a successful enterprise. Although many people look upon the beginning of a business as a milestone, it is only the first step. Next comes managing the business and guiding it toward profitability.

It is an unfortunate reality that most new businesses fail within the first three years. There are many reasons for companies not achieving sales expectations, but assuming that care was taken in evaluating the prospective company's market and that a viable market was found to exist, most can be traced to ineffective management. The company's marketing plan might be inadequate, resources might not be utilized in the most effective manner, or new clients might not be fully or properly pursued. As owner of your travel agency, effective management will be one of your prime responsibilities.

# Your Office

Effective management starts with your office. Setting up an efficient office in a designated area of your home will enable you to manage the operations of your travel agency more effectively. Working from your kitchen table is not only a sign of the unprofessional, it is likely to severely undermine your business efforts.

A home office should be set apart from the home's busy places – the kitchen, TV room, living room and other areas where traffic of relatives and children is high. Your office does not need to be big, but it should be large enough to work in comfortably, as well as possess good lighting, heat and air-conditioning, and appropriate furniture. If you decide to build an addition to your home or remodel a part of it, such as the basement or garage, you should check with local building authorities regarding zoning requirements or restrictions. You should also enlist the services of a professional builder who can help to ensure that the renovations and additions are constructed properly and according to local codes.

You have many choices where you might locate a home office. A spare bedroom, a den, a little-used family room or dining room, an enclosed porch, even a remodeled basement or garage can provide the space and comfort you need. While your office does not need to have the furnishings and equipment of the office of a Fortune 500 executive, you should have enough room to include the following:

- A desk and chair at which you can do paperwork and make phone calls. Your desk might include a fax machine, calculator, and other equipment. (Such items might also be positioned on another table or work area.)

- A computer workstation, including printer and Internet hookup.

- Space for filing cabinets and other storage containers.

- Shelves for storing books and office supplies.

- A table for assorted tasks such as preparing brochures for mailing.

- Optional – a small couch and table to meet with clients.

- If your office is small, you can store supplies and materials in the basement, garage, attic, or closets in other parts of your home.

There are many ways to create a professional appearance to your office. You might contact an interior decorator to help you achieve the type of office you want, or you can arrange the furnishings yourself. Following are some suggestions should you choose to set up your office yourself:

- Consider the amount of space you have. Avoid cramming so much furniture and equipment inside that you create a "cramped" feeling. If you have limited space, select essential items only.

- Consider your personality. Are you most comfortable in an airy, brightly-colored office, or do you work best in a rather plain, but functional environment? Think about the offices you have been in and which ones you like the best. You might also review office plans in décor magazines.

- Consider the "unity" of your office. Choose colors, style of furniture, and rugs that complement each other. The various items and furnishings in your office should all work together to create an impression of professionalism, reliability, and friendliness.

- Remember that the way you set your office up can affect your mood and productivity. A small, cramped office with old, worn furniture can quickly become depressing; however, a bright, office with new furniture arranged in a pleasing motif will boost your mood and output.

- When selecting furniture for your office, you must consider both comfort and appearance. Avoid big bulky desks and tables if your office is located in a small room. To form an idea of how you might furnish your office, sketch a plan of your office space and include the dimensions of walls, windows, and doorways. Study the plan and imagine furniture in various locations. Note the approximate size of furniture you might use. A six-foot long desk and four-foot long bookshelf, for example, will not fit along a nine-foot wall. Knowing the dimensions of the walls of your office before purchasing furniture can help you to avoid the unhappy prospect of trying to squeeze things into the places where they simply won't fit. A variety of desk styles and shapes are available and you should be able to find things that will "work" in your office. Always sit in chairs and at desks to determine if they are comfortable before you buy them. A visit to any office store that carries furniture will provide you with an assortment of pieces that will satisfy your needs.

- Select storage containers based on your needs and space. Always use existing storage areas first, for example shelves and closets in the room. Common storage containers include filing cabinets, bookshelves, storage bins, and wall units.

- Keep in mind that colors, too, can affect your mood. Bright, hot colors – reds and oranges, for example – have been found to boost moods, while cooler colors – such as blue and green – often provide a calmer, more relaxed atmosphere. Find the colors that work best for you.

- Wall and floor coverings should also be selected with care. Whether you choose paint or wallpaper for your walls, or tiles or carpeting for your floor, color and texture can make a powerful impression. Choose those coverings that make you feel most comfortable and which add to the overall environment of your office.

- No matter how you decorate your office, it will not be comfortable if you do not have efficient heat, air-conditioning, and ventilation. If necessary, contact a local heating/air-conditioning contractor to upgrade your system. This is especially true of offices located in basements and garages.

- Lighting must be of high quality. Select fixtures that provide plenty of "soft" light, which will help you to work at your peak efficiency without resulting in eyestrain.

Your office should be functional and professional, supporting your work in a comfortable setting. While a cramped, cluttered office can undermine your productivity, a clean, well-organized one can heighten your spirits and profits.

# Working Efficiently

While a professionally organized office will help you to conduct the activities of your travel agency effectively, it will still fall to you to do the work. Since you will likely be working alone, especially in the beginning, you must establish habits of efficiency, otherwise you risk becoming overwhelmed with the daily operations of your business. Meetings with prospective clients, phone messages, promotional activities, research, communications with a host agency, the ordinary paperwork of running a business – all can conspire to fill your time and bury you beneath demands.

Organization is the key to avoiding overload. You must develop a system in which everything has a time and place. Certainly computers make the task of organization easier, however, if you lack computer skills you should either obtain the skills necessary by attending a computer class or organize materials the old-fashioned way with pen, paper, and folders. Even with computers you will still have a need to file and store important papers, but most people at ease with computers appreciate the storage capacity of even a small system.

No matter how you decide to organize information, you should have various files: files for specific plans or programs you offer, files for clients, files for special subjects. Each file should contain the name(s) of the people involved, phone/ fax numbers, street and e-mail addresses, and any other pertinent information. You might also maintain a file containing "future" projects or ideas in which you store information regarding promotions or projects you might like to do during the upcoming months.

An effective method of storing the names and contact information about clients is with a Rolodex filing system or an electronic filer. Information is essential to the growth of your travel agency's client lists. A prospective client might not require your travel services this year, but he might be interested next. If you don't keep an accurate file on him, you won't be able to contact him and you might miss out on a sale.

As simple as a filing system is to keep – after all the only thing you must do is put each piece of information in its proper place – maintaining filing systems can be an exacting task.  Here are some tips to keep you on top of your files and not burdened beneath their weight:

- Each type of file should have a designated place. This might be in a file cabinet, a box on a shelf, or on a computer disk.  Note:  If you maintain files on the hard drive of your computer, be sure to keep accurate backup copies on floppy disks.  Some business owners keep at least two backups, at different locations.  In case of theft or some other unfortunate event that ruins one copy, the other copy will be safe.

- As soon as you are done with a file, place it in its designated spot.  Avoid putting it down on the corner of your desk and tell yourself you will put it away later.  Chances are you won't and you'll soon have files spread throughout your office.

- Place the most recent materials in the front of the file.

- Label all files.  If you are using folders, writing the name/subject on the top and along the side can make it easier to identify files quickly.

- Avoid filling files with so much material that they become unwieldy. Only file pertinent information and avoid jamming unnecessary data into files.

This will only make it harder to ascertain the most important material.

- Periodically, go through your files and weed out those that have become obsolete. For example, a company that has gone out of business will no longer require your travel services, although its owners or managers might in a new position. In this case, transfer the individuals to separate files of their own. Obsolete files that might someday yield information should be placed in storage. You should review your files at least once or twice a year. Files that are not regularly updated will not provide you with the quality information you need.

- Maintain files for business documents: contracts, insurance policies, and warranties.

- Store tax records for seven years. After completing your taxes, place the information in storage under the correct date.

Unquestionably, you must strive to achieve a level of high efficiency. You should prioritize and schedule your day so that you can complete the most important tasks first. Estimate how much time you will need to do something and plan accordingly. Be careful not to underestimate the time necessary for activities. If you underestimate consistently, you will always be falling behind and struggling to catch up.

This will only add to your stress and undercut your effectiveness. As a general rule, you should leave about 30% of your day unscheduled so that you will be able to attend to unexpected demands that arise. Follow the old adage: "Don't put off for tomorrow what you can do today."

Whenever possible, schedule meetings and make a strong effort to avoid unscheduled ones. Also, avoid scheduling unnecessary meetings. Don't, for example, schedule a meeting with someone when a phone call will achieve your purposes. Such meetings can waste significant amounts of time. Also, politely discourage people from walking in on you without an appointment. While a friend may be a valuable client, having him simply drop in on your office when you are meeting with another client, after which you have yet another appointment scheduled, is not an effective method of conducting business. You will probably find yourself rushing the other clients to meet with your friend, or you will feel pressured about having to meet with so many people in a short time frame. Rushed, hasty meetings seldom result in positive outcomes.

Any meeting you schedule should be planned. Before attending the meeting, decide what you wish to say and do. You might also wish to set a time limit to your meeting. While it is not wise to inform a potential client that you have allotted a certain length of time for him, having a time period in mind will help you to keep the meeting moving along and not digress onto trivial topics that will just waste your time.

Following are some tips to ensure that your meetings are effective:

- Set a time frame in advance for your meeting to begin and end.

- Create a plan of what you wish to discuss. If you are to meet with a potential client, gather materials that might help him decide on travel plans and help you to make a sale.

- Guide the meeting. Keep it on track according to your plan.

- Be conscious of the time frame you have allotted. Keep the meeting moving forward.

- Before ending the meeting, summarize the points that have been made. If the meeting involves a potential client, for example, and the client agrees to your travel plans, close the deal. If the client needs more time, note that you will contact him later and encourage him to contact you with any questions.

Daily operations, unless managed properly, can detract from your overall effectiveness just as much, and sometimes more, than poor scheduling. A cluttered desk, piled with days' old accumulation of mail, reports, and messages, can easily consume several hours that can be spent on contacting potential clients. Train yourself so that you acquire the habit of handling papers once. For example, after reading a letter, file it or place it in a tray from which you will respond to it. Simply letting it lie on a corner of the desk, one of a pile of other letters, only gives you the eventual task of resorting mail that has already been looked over. Any letter, report, or message that does not require a response or serve any purpose to satisfying your goals should be sent to the trash.

Some business owners write themselves a list of tasks that they wish to accomplish each day. Such daily planners can go a long way to keeping you on schedule and ensuring that you accomplish what must be done each day. If you do not finish your list, it is easy to carry over the unfinished activities to the next day. Planning lists help to keep you focused on your daily operations.

Never create a list, however, and feel that everything on it must be accomplished that particular day. You can expect unanticipated interruptions and should always be ready to deal

91

with them.  Of course, that will require you to move some of the day's scheduled activities to tomorrow.

When you plan your day, be cautious not to fill it with so many tasks that it will be impossible for you to achieve them all.  In time, such a practice will only make you feel that you are coming up short and not reaching your goals. While it is important that you conduct your business in an efficient manner, it is equally important that you allow yourself enough rest, relaxation, and exercise so that you remain in top form in mind and body.

To be most efficient your day must be well planned, and your activities should move you forward to achieving your goals.  At the end of the day, take a few minutes to review what you did.  Ask yourself what you feel went well and what you think you can improve.  Simple evaluation can often be of great aid in improving your management skills.

## Managing Your Phone

It is easy for small business owners to lose much time throughout the day because of the phone.  Because many small business owners do not have someone to answer the phone for them, they must either answer the phone when it rings or return messages. In either case, when a call is answered or returned, and it does not lead to a sale, time is lost.

To control your telephone time, you might rely on an answering machine. Obviously, there will be times when an interruption by a phone call will be counterproductive. Likewise, returning calls throughout the day will consume a large portion of your day and prove to be a distraction. You will probably find it most efficient to return calls either in the morning, before nine a.m., just before lunch, or toward the end of the workday. These are also the times you are most likely to connect with busy people. Set aside phone time and make the calls you must. This will leave the rest of the day for you to complete other work.

Another way to manage your phone is to set aside a specific time of the day when you receive and make calls. Letting associates know of your "phone time" helps to minimize calls that might otherwise disrupt other activities. Be careful with this, however, so that you don't give the impression that you are unapproachable.

To facilitate your phone time, always keep a message pad near your phone on which you can write down information. Whenever you are speaking with someone new, make certain that you obtain his or her name and phone number, and any other information you might require. Having a pad and pen handy makes it easy to write information down. Never try to "remember" names and phone numbers, intending to write them down later. You won't.

## Managing the Mail

Like your phone, you can easily become bogged down with mail. As with your phone, you will manage correspondence – both traditional mail and e-mail – most effectively if you set aside a specific time of the day to handle this part of your business.

You should manage your mail from a designated place in your office, perhaps a table or your desk. This should be the location at which you handle both incoming and outgoing mail. The materials you require for handling mail – stamps, mailing labels, envelopes, postage scale, letter opener, packaging tape, etc. – should be close by. Once you sit down to look through your mail, you should not have to get up and find stamps or tape. All the materials must be quickly accessible.

As you open your mail, you should also be sorting it. Immediately throw away "junk" mail. Correspondence that you need to respond to soon should be placed in one tray, bills in another, and other letters in a third. Designate shelf space for large packages.

You should build letter writing and responding to correspondence into your day. Right before or after lunch, or at the end of a day might be good times for you to write letters. E-mail should be sent during sessions when you are working at your computer. Always try to consolidate tasks that logically fit together.

You should also set up a schedule where you pay bills on a regular basis. Every Sunday night or perhaps every Friday morning will help you avoid the aggravation that comes with missing a payment and incurring late fees.

Unless managed effectively, mail can quickly become a burden to a small business. If you permit your mail to pile up, you will likely overlook some opportunities that can lead to additional sales. Mail management is an important part of a smooth-running operation.

# Avoiding "Underminers" of Efficiency

Working out of an office in your home provides many advantages. You will certainly enjoy lower overhead than if you rented office space, you can set your own hours, and you will be your own boss. You can set the pace of your work day and the level of your efficiency. However, there are many *underminers* of efficiency of which you must be aware and guard against. When working at home, it is easy to become distracted by a variety of sources and not put in the necessary hours and efforts to make your travel agency successful.

You must guard against the following:

- Chatting with neighbors and friends. While it might boost your overall efficiency to leave the office for a few moments, stroll in the backyard and breathe in some fresh air, talking with your neighbor over the back fence for a half-hour will not.

- Making personal phone calls on your "company's" time. Always remember that time in your office is time that you should be working. Personal phone calls – those not directly related to your business – will cost you more than the call itself.

96

- Taking the dog for an extended walk. Your dog may appreciate the extra attention, but you won't once you realize how your bottom line is suffering.

- Finding other jobs to do around the house. You might need to catch up on the wash, paint the family room, or weed the flower bed. While these all must get done, you should not do them when you should be working.

- Watching TV. You may enjoy a show that airs in the afternoon, but which comes at a time you should be working. Tape the show and watch it later.

- Taking an afternoon swim in the pool. You may convince yourself that this is a refreshing way to rejuvenate your energy, but you may wind up spending the rest of the day in the lawn chair and not in your office.

- Taking extended breaks. Be careful that coffee breaks don't extend through the morning and that lunch lasts well into the afternoon.

- Nursing minor illnesses. When you have to report to a job across town, it is sometimes easier to force yourself to go to work with a cold. When you work at home, it can be easier to simply lie in bed, telling yourself that you will sleep in a little longer and work later. You may wind up sleeping in but not working longer.

- Shortening your workday. Since you are working at home, it is easy to start your day later and end it earlier. After all, you are the boss. Unfortunately, this is not the way to build a successful business.

- Feeling a sense of alienation. Working at home, alone, is not for everyone. Some people need the interaction of others in an office environment to stimulate them and keep their creativity sharp. Without the interaction of others, these individuals may become depressed and lose their enthusiasm for their business. There are several steps you can take to relieve any feelings of alienation or loneliness. You should join community organizations, attend workshops and seminars in the travel industry, take college or evening classes that can enhance your business skills, and schedule regular meetings with potential clients.

- Losing motivation. Even people who can accept the challenge of working alone, can, over time, lose motivation. It can become difficult to put the necessary hours into a job when the job is at home amid many distractions. Those people working in offices in their home must constantly focus on their goals to keep moving forward.

- Overworking. Because the office is in your home, it is easy to work from early morning to late at night, especially since the more time you put in usually translates to more sales. While this may sound like a good strategy for success, remember that overwork will eventually result in stress and inefficiency. You must seek balance in your life. Setting up a reasonable schedule is one of the best ways to ensure that you work enough but not too much.

# Money Matters with Your Travel Agency

One of the first things you must do when establishing your travel agency is to create a financial "identity" for your new company. At its simplest, this includes opening a business bank account from which you can write checks and pay your travel agency's bills. A business account will enable you to keep all personal and company finances separate. You should also maintain all of your travel agency's financial materials and records in your office.

No matter how well you plan for the success of your travel agency, you should not expect to turn a profit for the first several months, and perhaps as long as the first few years.

You will need start-up money to sustain you through this period.

To ensure that they will not suffer great personal loss should their new business falter, many small business owners maintain another job while they are establishing their company. Keeping the day job provides the resources for the family's needs, and also relieves the owner from the pressure to make his company profitable as fast as possible. Extreme pressure and stress have caused many new business owners to make poor decisions regarding the growth of their companies, which in the end undermine the company's success. Establishing a company out of a home office, and maintaining another source of income, allows the owner to move slowly and build the company gradually. Such growth frequently leads to building a strong customer base and sound business practices that lead to future strength and profitability. In time, the owner quits the other job to concentrate entirely on his business.

Money management, without question, is a vital concern in any company. To manage money in your travel agency, you must create a budget. At the least, your budget should contain realistic projections of all the expenses you expect to incur. The budget should also include projections of anticipated income. Along with expected expenses and revenues, your start-up costs must also be accounted for in your first budget.

# Typical start-up costs include:

- Equipment costs.

- Deposits for utilities.

- Costs for phone/fax equipment.

- Costs for computer system and on-line fees.

- Fees for licenses.

- Costs for renovations, remodeling, etc.

In addition, you should include the monthly costs you expect, including:

- Telephone.

- Office supplies.

- Payments for any utilities.

- Postage.

- Publications.

- Miscellaneous fees.

Remember to total your expenses for the first several months, being ready to revise your estimates as you go along. Your budget should be flexible, a plan of money management and guidance that evolves as your business grows.

## Taxes and Deductions

While you will be required to pay taxes on the profits from your business, your home travel agency will also qualify for various tax deductions. Most importantly, to qualify for deductions, the IRS requires that you designate a portion of your home to be used exclusively for your business. While setting up your business on the kitchen table in the early going may be convenient, the IRS is likely to frown on your deducting expenses because they will question if indeed your travel business is a serious endeavor. After all, if it is serious, it should be operating out of an office. While your office does not have to be located in a separate room, it must be a space solely used by your company. In addition, your "office" must be your principal place of business or a place in which you meet with clients.

Once you have established your office in the eyes of the IRS, you will be able to deduct a variety of business expenses. It is because the deductions are so numerous that the IRS is strict with their definition of a home business, delineating it as opposed to a hobby or pastime. Establishing a true office is the measuring rod.

Under ordinary conditions, all expenses you incur while conducting or improving your business will be tax deductible. Be sure to file all receipts and keep all canceled checks so that you can justify your expenses at tax time. Here is a common list of expenses you will likely be able to deduct:

- Costs for office equipment.

- Costs for improvements to your office – painting, the addition of carpeting, new wiring for your computer system, new lighting, etc. Those improvements that are considered to be capital improvements are depreciated, which means that the deduction is spread over time.

- Costs for mortgage, utilities, insurance, etc. are deductible according to the area your office occupies in relation to the overall house. If, for example, your office occupies one-sixth of the total area of your home, you can deduct a sixth of the above expenses, provided the deduction does not exceed the gross income of your travel agency.

- Costs associated with operating your business such as –

  - office supplies

  - telephone and on-line services

  - accounting, attorney, and other professional services

  - advertising and promotion fees

  -  bank service charges and interest on loans

  - license fees

  - taxes

  - postage and shipping

  - travel

  - consulting services

  - commissions paid to other agents

  - books, periodicals, and journals

- membership in professional groups

- seminars, workshops, and continuing education.

Note, these are just some of the more common deductions. Virtually any cost that arises from the operations of your travel agency will be deductible.

Because deductions can save your travel agency substantial money at tax time, it will be to your benefit to consult a tax specialist or accountant experienced with small, home businesses. Your fees will be returned to you several times over in tax savings.

While the success of a business is often a result of hard work, you can increase the chances for your travel agency's success through competent management. When you develop daily routines and procedures that are efficient and effective, you will maximize your efforts and improve the chances for your travel agency to grow.

# Providing Travel Services

If setting up a travel agency can be described as challenging, making your agency profitable is truly a daunting task that requires hard work and persistence. However, it can be done and the rewards will pay back your efforts many times over.

Perhaps the most important bricks of the foundation on which any successful business is built is its personnel. Even if you are operating your business alone, you will need the help, advice, and expertise of others.

You will undoubtedly find that an attorney experienced in small business is essential to your travel agency. Not only will you need to consult your attorney over your initial business plan, but your attorney will become a key individual to the success of your travel agency. He will help you to draft and sign essential documents and contracts, and he will offer you his advice when you need a legal opinion. Your attorney will also help you to file any necessary documents and obtain any certifications from federal, state, and local authorities you may need so that your travel agency operates fully within the law. Of course, should you require his services during litigation, he will stand beside you. The counsel of a wise attorney should never be dismissed.

Your accountant is another vital member of your team. It is his responsibility to manage your travel agency's finances. An accountant knowledgeable in the operations of small businesses, and particularly travel agencies, can be a superb asset to your growing business by helping you manage cash flow.

Your bank is also a critical element in your march to profitability. There will be times when you will need access to cash – perhaps for capital investment or perhaps to help you through a slow period. Having a bank that is understanding of and responsive to your needs and goals can help you sustain your growth in spite of unexpected obstacles. If possible, you should develop a relationship with one of your bank's representatives who has the authority to grant you the accessibility you need. Many large banks maintain staffs that work individually with businesses, including small start-ups, and you should seek out this kind of relationship.

Although he may not be thought of immediately when you consider individuals essential to the success of your business, your insurance agent is a man you should consult during the establishment of your agency. Even if your office is located in your home, you will need insurance for your business against loss from fire, storms, theft, and accidents. Anyone who comes to your office and who might trip or fall or in any way be injured while on the premises can sue you for damages. Liability insurance is essential protection. If you hire employees, you must acquire and maintain Workmen's Compensation. You should also consider business interruption insurance, which will provide a monetary cushion in the event that some catastrophe – perhaps an illness striking you or the coming of a natural disaster – interrupts the operation of your travel agency and reduces your cashflow. While you might be able to obtain adequate coverage at a fair price from your insurance agent, he or she might not be able to provide you with the coverage you need. Thus, you should shop around for the most comprehensive coverage at the best price. Be sure to consult your attorney in regard to matters of insurance.

Along with your attorney, accountant, bank, and insurance agent, there will be many other people with whom you will develop on-going relationships which will benefit your business. You might, for example, buy your computer equipment from a local dealer who also provides service should your equipment malfunction. Working with local providers can often result in the personal touch lacking from the major outlets.

Once your travel agency is established, it is probable that you will need to hire staff, either full- or part-time. Seek individuals who are experienced, competent, and with whom you feel comfortable. If you cannot find people with a lot of travel experience, look for those who exhibit a willingness to work hard and learn. Sometimes, the people who learn their trade with a company become its most valuable employees.

Although you may surround yourself with qualified people who can help your business grow, profitability and true success will be elusive if you fail to offer the products and services the public desires. Providing travel products and services at fair prices clearly is the most important factor for success.

## Your Travel Products and Services

As a business owner it is your decision which products and services your travel agency will offer. You might offer numerous products and services, or you might limit your offerings, focusing on just a few and striving to outmarket and outsell your competition in selected areas. Limiting your offerings helps you to specialize, but it also reduces your potential client base. Determining which travel products and services to offer is not an easy decision.

Most travel agencies offer a variety of the most common products and services, including:

- Airline tickets.

- Car rentals.

- Reservations for hotels, motels, and bed and breakfast inns.

- Reservations for resorts.

- Cruises.

- Tours.

- Transportation via rail, bus, motorcoach.

- Passport photos.

Most potential clients will desire at least one, and usually several of the above. Providing a client with multiple services and products will enhance your profits.

Following is a discussion about each of the products and services listed above.


# Airline Tickets


If you are like most travel agents who work out of an office in their home, you will work closely with a host agency to obtain airline ticket reservations for your clients. The obvious question now becomes: If you are enlisting the services of a host agency, why doesn't the client simply go to the other agency and not bother doing business with you? Even if not asked outright, the question is on the minds of many clients. After all, travelers these days can merely consult their own computer to access airline ticket information.

While that may sound easy – and in some cases it is – in many cases the potential client winds up spending a significant amount of time on his computer accessing information regarding tickets and prices, and he is not always sure he is getting the best price and the most practical arrangements. In those cases he does get the best price, his departure time may be in the small hours of the morning, or he may have to fly out of his way and change planes two or three times before arriving at his destination. The price might be right, but little else in this rather common scenario is.

Your greatest value lies in that you can provide airline tickets at the most reasonable price along with a suitable flight. The service you sell to potential clients is not only the airline ticket, but your expertise. You can help your clients find the best tickets and best accommodations within their budgets that satisfy their travel needs. Not only will your service likely save them money, it will certainly save them the time of searching for the best travel deals – which they are probably not going to find on their own.

One of the most serious problems travelers who book their own flights face occurs when their flight is canceled. At such unhappy times, they are usually forced to rely on the airline's ticket personnel to rebook their flight, a difficult prospect even under the best of conditions. It is for this reason that many thoughtful travelers rely on travel agents. When they find themselves stranded, these individuals call their travel agents who can often find them another flight sooner and more efficiently than airline personnel can. Such acts make for loyal clients. Whenever you are attempting to sell your travel services to any client, you should emphasize that you stand by your clients and are always ready to assist them in any travel dilemma.

Your personal touch and expertise also manifest when you share with potential clients your knowledge of their destinations and your suggestions that will help to make their trip more enjoyable. When clients realize that you can make their trip easier and less costly, they will be happy to buy your products and services.

# Car Rentals

Your services should not end when your client reaches his or her destination, but should extend throughout his or her trip. Car rentals are not only essential for many travelers, but they are profitable for you. Vacationers may require rental cars to view the sights of their destinations, while business travelers need cars to travel to their meetings.

In most cases, you will earn a commission of up to 10% on every car you arrange for your clients to rent. This can add up to a substantial, and steady, income for your agency. To arrange for car rentals effectively, you must become familiar with the various car rental companies in the destinations of your clients. You must become knowledgeable regarding rates, conditions, and types of cars your clients may rent. This can take quite some research if your clients travel to various destinations, but it is necessary if you hope to present your clients with the best automobiles at the most economical rates. The rates and offerings of car rental companies differ throughout the world, and your clients will appreciate your "steering" them in the right direction.

Some clients, those who wish to travel through Europe on their own, for example, might prefer to buy a car there, use it for their trip, and then bring it home. For extended stays that include automobile travel, purchasing a car overseas can lead to big savings over renting. You should offer the service of arranging for the purchase of a car for your clients. Specialized car dealerships regularly handle such sales and offer fair prices and reliable delivery. As with providing rentals, your commission from such sales can be well worth your efforts.

Most profitable travel agencies offer car rental and purchase services. The typical client appreciates this service.

# Hotels, Motels, Resorts, and Bed and Breakfast Inns

Arranging for the accommodations of your clients will be a major source of your income. Most hotels, motels, and inns pay a commission of up to 10% to travel agents for booking guests. Note that some establishments, particularly foreign hotels, pay less and you should always inquire about the commission schedule of any hotel, motel, or inn before booking clients.

Because the perceptions of hotels and motels are sometimes fuzzy in the minds of clients, a few definitions will serve them well:

- A hotel most often caters to vacationers and business travelers. Hotels might be small, containing only a few dozen rooms, or they might be several stories high and contain hundreds of rooms.

- A motel most often caters to individuals and families who travel by car. Many motel guests stay a night only –- because they are enroute to their destination – or a few nights, but seldom longer. Some motels can be quite large and have a hundred or more rooms.

- A resort offers accommodations near amusements and entertainment. Many resorts provide a variety of activities and services for their guests. An individual can typically spend his or her entire vacation at a major resort and not run out of things to do. Resorts are usually large and have hundreds of rooms.

- Bed and breakfast inns are often restored "grand" homes that can provide travelers with overnight stays, and breakfast, lunch, and dinner. They offer a "homey" atmosphere in picturesque, period settings. Rooms are usually decorated in historic or regional themes, providing a relaxed, delightful atmosphere.

In addition to understanding the basics of accommodations, you also must be aware of the various rating systems that classify establishments at which your clients might stay. Following is a rundown of the most common:

- Budget – basic services with few amenities. Cost is less expensive in comparison to other establishments. A similar designation is "third class" or "economy."

- First class – plenty of amenities and "extras." Cost can be high, but generally the clients preferring "first class" appreciate the quality services. A similar designation is "deluxe."

- The star system – a five-star designation is the highest.  Stars decrease to a one-star accommodation, which is equivalent to budget class.

While some of your clients will know where they wish to stay while traveling, many will welcome your advice on accommodations.  To ensure that you are able to assist your clients in choosing the accommodations that will satisfy their desires as well as their wallets, you must be fully knowledgeable in the accommodations available in the destination of your clients.  Here, again, research is critical. Travel agents who are able to provide potential clients with valuable information are more likely to close the sale than those can offer clients few facts and insights.

Because the range of accommodations in most cities is so broad, your clients will have plenty of places at which they might stay. Before recommending any place, you should ascertain what type of accommodations your clients might be considering.  Some people will know that they wish to stay in a budget hotel; others will want to travel first class through their entire trip; many will fall between these two categories.

Most clients will base their decision on accommodations on several factors, including:

- Money.

- Personal preferences.

- Business considerations.

- Recreations.

- Special events or activities.

In most cases, you should avoid trying to talk a client into accommodations that he or she may be uncomfortable with, even if you believe that the accommodations would, in the end, be more satisfying. You might offer such accommodations as a suggestion, but if the client prefers somewhere else, accept his or her desire.

Along with helping them to find satisfying accommodations, most clients find it helpful if you provide them with information that will make their trip more enjoyable. You might for example, offer the following kinds of information:

- Meal plans. Some hotels and resorts offer meal plans that can save vacationers money, especially if they are traveling with children. Many hotels and motels offer complimentary breakfasts.

- Special activities, events, or celebrations.

- Special sites to visit.

- Free services, for example, shuttle service. Such services are often provided by large resorts.

- Baby-sitting services or special activities for children.

- Tips about the weather and suggestions as to the type of clothing to bring.

- Any type of information that will make the trip or stay more enjoyable and hassle-free.

You can learn about the services and accommodations offered by hotels, motels, resorts, and inns through their guides, brochures, and manuals. You should make research into accommodations a regular part of your travel agency's operations.

# Cruises

Cruises provide a large portion of the income of many travel agencies. A variety of cruises are available for a variety of potential clients. Typical cruise lines ply the Caribbean, Mediterranean, Alaska, Scandinavia, and the Orient. Cruise ships regularly visit some of the most exciting ports in the world, including Bermuda and the Bahamas. Cruises may be designed to cater to a specific client – honeymooners, "singles," seniors, families, and, of course, business people who are on the cruise to attend workshops and seminars.

As with land-based accommodations, cruises vary greatly in their amenities and rates. Although the general protocols are much the same, different ships provide different activities. Certainly their destinations are a major interest for potential travelers.

In order to help your clients most effectively, you need to know about the major cruise lines, their ports of call, quality of service, and staff. While some ships offer a somewhat formal and elegant atmosphere, others are more casual. Some ships offer numerous special activities for children and cater to families, while others design their itineraries primarily for adults. When helping clients select a cruise that they will find pleasurable and affordable, you must uncover what their desires and expectations are and match them to the appropriate ship.

You should also offer information about the ship and cruise your clients select. You might explain the following:

- General protocols and accepted behaviors.

- Cabins – size, type, location.

- Destinations and ports of call.

- Attire.

- Special activities.

- Special considerations of which travelers need to be aware.

To explain a cruise with enthusiasm and from the perspective of experience, you should take as many familiarization trips as possible. This will supply you with firsthand knowledge of what the ship offers and the overall value of the cruise. Obviously, it is not possible to have sailed on every cruise potential clients may ask you about. If this is the case, provide the client with as much information that you do have – brochures, pamphlets, etc. – and offer to find out more information.  Any time you promise to find out information for a client, be sure that you send along the information as quickly as possible.  This will enhance your image in the eyes of the client and help to secure a sale.

Like other services you provide, cruise lines pay you when you book clients on their ships.  Because of their popularity, cruises can be a significant portion of your yearly income.

# Tours

Tours provide excellent income for many travel agencies. Most tours are pre-packaged, meaning that they are sold by tour operators and have a set of destinations, sites, and and events. Your primary task in the selling of a tour package is to match the needs and desires of your client with the appropriate tour.

A vast variety of tours are available, many of which may be designed with optional routes and activities suited to a client's satisfaction.  Typical tours include:

- An overland tour of Europe.

- Bicycling tours through parts of Europe.

- Ski trips to Rocky Mountain resorts.

- Ski trips to the Alps.

- Sailing tours to ports of the Mediterranean.

- Sailing tours to ports of the Caribbean.

- African safaris.

- Religious tours of the Middle East.

- Tours of Australia and the Outback.


Tours are popular among vacationers because tours not only visit numerous places, but they also include special activities and events at packaged prices that are usually much more reasonable than if the traveler attempted to follow the tour on his or her own.  The standard tour offers a memorable experience for a fair price. You, of course, benefit from the commissions you earn by arranging tours.

To sell tours effectively, you must be able to provide clients with as much useful information as possible. Most tour operators provide brochures and pamphlets that describe their tours fully, including pricing, and you should obtain as much material as you can. If possible, take the tour yourself so that you can describe your experiences to your clients. Many tour operators are willing to offer travel agents steep discounts in hopes that the agent will direct travelers their way.

## The Bus Tour

Tours by bus, also referred to as motorcoach, may be lengthy, and visit sites throughout a region or country, or they may be rather short, only a day or two, and visit one or two sites. The destination of a bus tour may be a particular city, a historic site, a celebration, or an event. Whichever the purpose for the tour, bus tours can be easily arranged through local or regional transportation companies and can command high commissions. Many companies that handle bus tours also include guides who provide information about the sites visited.

Some transportation companies will prefer to pay you a flat rate. In such cases, your profits are derived from selling seats on the bus. Your profits are therefore based on your filling of the bus, and you must be diligent in selling enough seats to earn a profit. Overall, however, bus tours to desirable sites and events tend to be profitable for travel agents, particularly if the agent books overnight stays at motels or hotels.

# Railways

Travel by railroads is yet another mode of transportation that can lead to significant profits for your travel agency. Although rail travel in the United States, except for Amtrak, is not as popular or common as it is in Europe, rail travel is still an option for many travelers. Sleeping accommodations can be arranged, and the dining experience can be quite pleasurable. For travelers who are journeying a distance of a few hundred miles, rail travel is often a more practical choice than travel by car or plane. The commissions you receive from arranging seats for rail travel can be significant.

# Selling Passport Photographs

The selling of passport photographs can generate both traffic and profit for your travel agency. Any client to whom you sell travel services and who requires a passport photo is a candidate for your photo service. If you can take a simple photo of a person, you can offer passport photographs.

If you prefer, you might enlist the services of a professional photographer whose studio is nearby. You would need to split the fee with him, perhaps by arranging for a commission for every client you send to him. While you would earn less per client, you would free yourself from having to work with the photographs. Under this agreement, you can offer your clients a valuable service and the photographer gains business. Everyone wins – you provide a service to your clients and gain a commission, the photographer receives customers for which he does not have to advertise, and your clients are freed from having to find a reliable photographer from whom to obtain their passport photos.

# The Effective Use of Travel Brochures

Virtually all travel service providers – tour and cruise operators, resort management, the staffs at hotels, motels, and inns – will provide you with brochures with which you can persuade potential clients to choose their offerings over the offerings of competitors. Brochures can, without question, make your selling of travel services easier. It is essential that you use brochures in the most effective manner. Following are some suggestions:

- Obtain brochures from as many travel service providers as possible. Review them regularly and become familiar with their offerings. If possible, visit some of the sites or take some of the cruises and tours. In many cases, familiarization trips can be inexpensive, fun, and informative. They will also help you to speak like a travel authority from firsthand experience.

- Always discuss the needs and desires of your clients first. After ascertaining the client's travel goals, select three or four brochures that might help him decide which trip or plan to take. Try to choose brochures that truly match the client's interests. Offering random brochures that do not meet the needs of your client will quickly brand you as an individual willing to sell any services, whether or not they are what your client wants. You risk losing business with this tactic.

- Avoid offering brochures with which you are unfamiliar. You won't sound genuine or knowledgeable in talking about the places they describe and you might seem incompetent.

- If possible, sit on the same side of the table as your client when looking at a brochure, or at least in a position so that you can view the brochure together. Merely handing the client the brochure will enable him to browse through it and ignore what you are saying. It is better for you to explain the brochure and share your knowledge about the places it describes.

- Never read the contents of a brochure to your client. He can read and will probably resent your reading to him.

- Use highlighting pens to circle or underscore major points of interest in the brochure.

- Be ready to answer any questions the client may have. If you are unsure of something, inform your client that you will find out and contact him as soon as you do. Never guess and mistakenly give the client erroneous information.

- If the client does not purchase travel services this day, permit him to take the brochures with him. Be sure to staple your business card to the brochure, making it easy for the client to call you. In a few days, if he doesn't call you, call him to follow up your meeting. Ask if he has any further questions and if you can be of additional help.

- Never give brochures out without explaining them. Clients may simply take them home and forget about them.

Incorporate brochures with your selling techniques. As support materials, brochures can help place colors and sights in your client's imagination and make your job of selling travel services easier.

# Payment Procedures

Establishing effective payment procedures is crucial to the success of your travel agency. Even though you may in some cases be providing services for people you know, a clear and practical payment policy is necessary.

Make your payment policy easily available and never hesitate to discuss costs and payment should a client inquire. When a client contracts with you, explain the method of payment and terms of credit.

For most travel agents, a major credit card is the preferred form of payment. Credit card transactions offer benefits to both you and your client, including:

- You do not have to extend credit; the credit card issuer does.

- You incur less risk. Checking credit availability is a simple procedure.

- You enjoy a seven-day ticket payment cycle.

- Your client receives excellent credit terms. Most credit cards have a grace period of between 20 and 30 days.

- Your client does not have to pay cash.

- For both of you, the transaction is simplified.

To establish credit card procedures, contact the credit card companies for information.

Consider the following advice regarding payment policies:

- Accept cash.

- Accept credit cards payments (provided the card is valid and has enough available credit).

- Accept checks but always make sure that they clear your bank before you provide any tickets or finalized services.

- Never provide services without some form of payment.

- If a client asks for services with the promise of sending a check tomorrow, politely inform him that your payment policy does not permit such transactions.

# Payment and Corporate Clients

Corporate clients will expect to be treated differently under your payment policy than individuals. Unlike the vacationing couple who will likely pay for travel services with their credit card, the corporate client will more likely pay for travel services at the end of the month. Corporations and businesses can, clearly, be a lucrative addition to your client base, however, you must be careful to ensure proper payment.

If you are like most travel agents, you will find that many companies pay their bills in a timely and professional manner, while, unfortunately, some others routinely delay until the twelfth hour or will frequently ignore requests for payment – especially from small companies. Large, mid-sized, and small companies can all be guilty of paying their bills slowly. Perhaps this is due to a corporate decision, or it might simply be due to sloppy bookkeeping. The result for you, however, is the same – you suffer from snail-pace payments.

To reduce the risk of slow-paying corporations and businesses, always request credit references from new companies. A typical credit check includes at least the name of the potential client's bank and the names of at least three credit references. Be sure to contact all of them. If a company is reluctant to provide references, or if the references indicate that the company is slow in paying its bills, you might be wise not to extend credit.

Once you have accepted a company as a client, be sure to monitor its account regularly. This will help you to spot any late payments. Should you find a company falling behind in its payments, call and find out why they are late. Perhaps the payment was mailed and it has been delayed in the mail (this really does happen once in a while), or the payment was overlooked. In such cases, ask for payment to be sent immediately and it usually will be. Sometimes, however, a company experiences slowed sales or financial setbacks and can not pay all of its bills. While the phone bill, heating bill, and electrical bills might be paid on time, the bills due small travel agencies may be ignored. If this unfortunate event occurs, you must call, perhaps frequently, to make certain that you remain in the minds of the individuals who are paying the bills. Be wary of providing more services if past services have not been paid for.

Following are some tips for collecting past due bills:

• Be polite but persistent in your collecting efforts.

- Written reminders and polite phone calls will help to remind people that you have not been paid for your services.

- When calling, ask to speak to the head of the department. Speaking with a secretary or – even worse – leaving a message on an answering machine will do little good.

- When speaking with individuals about unpaid bills, be gracious and professional. Inform them that the bill is unpaid, that you have enjoyed providing travel services for the company in the past, and hope to be able to continue to do so.

Collecting overdue bills from companies that have a history of reluctance when it comes to paying their bills, or companies that have suffered financial setbacks, can be a difficult and unpleasant task. For this reason alone, you should perform the necessary credit checks before providing services to business clients.

# Ticket Delivery

If possible, arrange to have your clients pick up their tickets in person. However, if you must mail tickets, you should use certified/registered mail, which requires a signature upon delivery. You may also purchase postal insurance in the event the tickets become lost. The costs for such mail service should be added into the fees you charge your clients. Although the cost for certified/registered mail is higher than first class postage, the added safety it provides is well worth the price. You might instead use an overnight delivery service, but even here you should require the signature of the individual receiving the delivery.

The success of your travel agency will be determined in large part by the success you have in providing travel services. Establishment of efficient and effective management of your operations is essential if your agency is to achieve profitability.

# Booking Travel Services

Booking travel services is the heart of your travel agency's business. It is through bookings that you gain your income, and it will be your bookings that ultimately determine whether your travel agency will attain profitability. If you are to become successful, you must commit much of your effort to booking travel services for your clients. Selling services is the preliminary step to booking; it is through booking that the deal is consummated.

Accurate record-keeping should be one of your primary concerns when booking travel services. Not only should you compile detailed information about each of your clients, but you need to record their travel destinations and any information that helps you to identify their travel needs. Furthermore, you need to maintain precise records that detail your actual bookings with airlines, cruise lines, tour operators, and places for accommodations.

You should start with your clients. Every client you have should have his or her own Data Sheet. While such sheets vary from agency to agency, most share many common elements. A basic Client Data Sheet should include information such as the following:

- Name.

- Street address.

- E-mail address.

- Telephone and (if applicable) fax number. If possible, you should obtain both day and evening phone numbers where your client can be reached. A caution here: Avoid calling your client at work unless your client tells you that you may.

- Notes regarding travel objectives and preferences. These might include the types of accommodations the client prefers, the types of automobiles he likes to rent, the class of airline he enjoys flying, and the kinds of resorts he likes to visit.

- Credit card information.

- Any special information that will help you to satisfy the client's travel goals and needs.

Client Data Sheets can be maintained on standard 8- by 11 1/2-inch paper or 4- by 6-inch note cards. Standard sheets of paper can be stored in folders and file cabinets, and note cards can be stored in card cases. Clients should be arranged alphabetically according to last names for quick access. Comprehensive Data Sheets provide you with fast information about clients and also serve as the basis of mailing lists. Your Data Sheets should be easy to access so that you can pull and refer to them whenever a client contacts you.

An important consideration regarding Client Data Sheets is privacy. Many people these days are concerned with privacy. Should any client ask you about your privacy policy, assure him that any information you maintain about him in your files is confidential. This requires that you do not share information about the client with any outside agency or organization. Your clients will appreciate your consideration.

Along with maintaining accurate information about your clients, you must make sure that you keep precise records regarding bookings. Most travel agencies log the greatest amount of their time booking airline flights, car rentals, reservations for accommodations, tours, and bus and rail tickets. The process is much the same for all, but with some important variations.

# Booking Airline Tickets

Booking airline tickets for your clients will probably be one of your most common services. Whether you book the tickets with airlines yourself or book them through a host agency, you must be meticulous in your work to ensure that all is correct. Following the steps below can help you book airline tickets efficiently.

- Record all pertinent information. You should create a Client Airline Data Sheet, on which you can write the name, address, and phone number of your client, specific airline information, including the name of the airline, flight number, place of departure, time of departure, place of arrival, and time of arrival. You should also include the ticket number, cost, and payment. At the bottom of the sheet you should leave space for special notes.

- When a client contacts you about obtaining airline tickets, use an Airline Data Sheet to record all necessary information. In addition to the information noted above, ask the client if he is traveling alone or if others are traveling with him. If yes, find out how many. Also ask if he prefers a particular airline, if he has accumulated any frequent flyer bonuses, and find out which class he prefers to travel, for example, first class, business, or coach.

- Find out what type of fare the client needs such as senior citizen, child, etc.

- Find out if the client has any medical conditions that will require special assistance from the airline's staff. (You should become familiar with the various guidelines of airlines regarding medical disabilities and concerns. Their guidelines vary somewhat.)

- Find out if the client needs special considerations because of small children. (Children under the age of five are not permitted to fly unaccompanied in the U.S., and those under eight are not permitted on flights in which they must change planes.)

- Find out if the client requires special meals.

- Find out if the client will be carrying any special luggage and will need any other special assistance.

- In cases where the client is flying to a foreign country, check if he or she has the necessary visas and passport. Help the client obtain them if necessary. A simple call to the airline or the destination country's embassy can usually provide you with all the information.

- Ask if the client would like you to book accommodations or a rental car.

- Always ask if you can be of any additional service.

When you call an airline to book tickets, the ticket reservationist will require a variety of information. Having a completed Airline Data Sheet will enable you to provide the following information easily.

- Place of departure.

- Destination.

- Date(s) of travel.

- Time of travel.

- Class of service requested.

- Type of fare requested.

- Name(s) of passengers.

- Telephone number of client.

- Your telephone number.

- Any special requests.

Once you have provided the reservationist with the above, you should obtain the following from him or her:

- Locator Number.

- Total amount of the costs for each person.

- Flight information.

- The airline reservationist's agent sine.

Be sure to record this information so that you can refer to it in the event of a flight cancellation or unexpected problem.

Whenever booking airline tickets, collect the payment from the client in advance, either by credit card or check. In the case of checks, make sure that the check clears your bank before the client picks up his tickets.

Once you have booked reservations for clients, you should monitor the status of their tickets. Sometimes airlines will lower fares in an effort of promoting business, and you might be able to arrange for your clients to pay the lower fare. If a fare reduction that might affect some of your clients occurs, call the airline and check to see if, indeed, your clients are due a refund. If they are, make the necessary arrangements and inform your clients. Protecting your clients' interests in this manner will be appreciated and will result in generating good will and new business for your agency.

Along with monitoring airline ticket prices, you must be ready to act if clients need to cancel their ticket reservations or if they lose tickets they have already picked up. The various airlines maintain their own policies regarding these situations, and you should contact the individual airline when such an event occurs. You should also always be ready to assist clients in the event their flight is canceled. Helping them to get on another flight quickly and conveniently will result in loyal customers.

Because the sale of airline tickets will comprise a major part of your travel agency's revenues, you must learn as much as you can about the various policies and procedures of booking flights. Expert knowledge will enable you to satisfy the airline needs of your clients. Always remember that people seek the services of travel agents so that their travel is made easier. Satisfy the needs of your clients and they will return to you for future trips.

# Reserving Accommodations

Just as important as booking airline flights, making reservations at hotels, motels, resorts, and inns will account for a large part of your business. To ensure that you obtain the necessary information from your clients when they call requesting that you make reservations for their stay while on their trip, you should create a Client Accommodation Data Sheet. Similar to the Client Airline Data Sheet, this sheet will enable you to record all the necessary information regarding a client's hotel, motel, resort, or inn preferences and needs.

While Accommodation Data Sheets may vary somewhat, the following information should be recorded:

- Client's name.

- Client's address and phone number.

- Name or type of establishment at which he wishes to stay. Perhaps the client prefers to stay at a particular chain or resort. (If he knows the name of the establishment, include its address and phone number.)

- Location of the place the client would like to stay, including area – near the beach, close to an airport, in the heart of the city.

- Location of room – first floor, overlooking the marina, near the pool, etc.

- Price range.

- Eligibility for special discounts or rates – senior citizens, children staying for free, etc.

- Type of accommodations – single, double, suite, etc.

- Preferred status, if any.

- Check-in date with estimated arrival time.

- Guaranteed late arrival time, if applicable.

- Check-out date with estimated departure time.

- Special considerations, if any.

After obtaining the necessary information, you should contact the establishment and make the reservations. Once you do, record the following on the Client's Accommodations Data Sheet:

- Name of the establishment (hotel, motel, resort, or inn.) Your sheet should also include the address of the establishment and its phone number (preferably an 800 number).

- Arrival time.

- Departure time.

- Type of accommodations and location.

- Price.

- Special considerations.

- Confirmation number.

After you have confirmed the reservation, inform your client and note if a guaranteed reservation has been arranged. Explain any details that can make your client's stay more enjoyable. If for any reason a client later calls you to cancel his reservation, do so immediately so that your client is not charged for a room he does not occupy.

# Booking Cruises

For most travel agencies, the booking of cruises provides for significant income.  As the popularity of cruises has increased in recent years among various segments of the population, cruises have become the main avenue of profits for many travel agents.  They can, without question, become a major source of income for you.

Cruises come in all forms and durations.  Some cruises skirt the islands of the Caribbean for a few days, stopping in only a port or two, while others sail around the world for months at a time.  Some cruises are designed around special themes – honeymooners, singles, seniors, self-help workshops and seminars, or young adult getaways.  Some cruises sail with holiday festivities – a Christmas/New Year's cruise to the islands for example.  The typical cruise offers numerous activities and amenities – swimming, health club, shuffleboard, aerobics, shopping, entertainment, and a movie threater are just a few among the many — plenty of fine food, music, dancing, and quality service by pleasant and well-mannered staff.

Because cruises come in so many forms, you must create a Client Cruise Data Sheet on which you can record specific information that will help you match your clients to the cruise that is just right for them. Your Client Cruise Data Sheet should consist of the following:

- Client's name.

- Client's address and phone number.

- Desired area of cruise, for example, the Caribbean, Alaska, or the Far East.

- Desired ports of call, if any.

- Number of people in client's party. Note if children will be present.

- Length of cruise.

- General time period for which the client would like to take the cruise.

- Desired level of service and amenities.

- Desired types of activities.

- Desired type and location of cabin.

- Preferred types of meals.

- Preferred seating arrangements.

- Price range.

- Desire for smoking or non-smoking rooms and areas.

After you have obtained the above information, you should discuss with your client the choices he has in cruise lines and specific cruises. In many cases, clients who are trying to keep within a budget will need to revise their expectations, however, most clients will be rather easy to satisfy because most cruises offer so many amenities and entertainments. Keep in mind that most cruises are booked well in advance, in many cases several months and sometimes up to a year or more.

Once your client selects a particular cruise, call the cruise line and book the reservations. Be sure that you make the reservations in accordance with the client's preferences. At this time, the reservationist will inform you whether rooms are still available and at what price. If you cannot obtain what the client wishes, check with him before completing the reservations. You should also obtain a cabin number and a confirmation number.

150

After making the reservations, contact your client and inform him of the particulars. On the Client Cruise Data Sheet, you should include information regarding the final costs and considerations.

## Booking Tours

The booking of tours is yet another lucrative service for your travel agency. Because tour operators plan the schedule, destinations, and activities of their tours – frequently including airline tickets — your work is often reduced to matching your clients with the tour that they will find most enjoyable. To help you provide your clients with the best of tour experiences, create a Client Tour Data Worksheet that includes the following:

- Client's name.

- Client's address and phone number.

- Preference for type and place of tour.

- Preference for dates.

151

- Preferred activities, sites, or events.

- Price range.

- Preference for meal plan.

Once you have obtained the ecessary information from your client, you should provide him with tour choices. Upon selecting a tour, you must contact the tour operator, who will inform you of the availability of the tour, costs, and details. You must then inform your client of schedules and requirements. If necessary, book airline reservations so that your clients will meet with their tour guides on time.

# Making Reservations for Car Rentals

To enable you to record vital information regarding reservations for car rentals, you should create a Client Car Rental Data Sheet. This sheet should be similar to other data sheets and should include:

- Client's name.

- Client's address and phone number.

- Location, date, and time of pick-up of the rental vehicle.

- Location, date, and estimated time the rental car will be returned to the rental agency.

- Client's preference of car rental company.

- Client's preference of make and type of car (for example, Ford, mid-sized, four-door, blue).

- Client's preference for automatic or standard transmission.

- Price range.

- Any special considerations or needs your client may have.

After you have obtained information from your client you should contact the car rental agency directly and make the reservation. Be sure to obtain a confirmation number. Once you have completed the reservation, call your client and inform him of the location he can pick the car up and the location where he can drop the car off. Should your client later have to cancel his trip and the use of the rental car, call the company promptly and cancel his reservation.

# Reservations for Bus and Motorcoach

While booking bus and motorcoach travel for clients generally comprises a smaller part of the operations of most travel agencies, these services still can add to your monthly income. In some cases, they can become quite profitable, especially if you develop a client base that enjoys this type of travel.

To ensure that you meet the needs of your clients in traveling by bus or motorcoach, you should create a Client Bus and Motorcoach Data Sheet. You should record the following information on the sheet:

- Client's name.

- Client's address and phone number.

- Number of people in client's party, with notation of the number of children.

- Destination.

- Place from which they are leaving.

- Departure time and estimated arrival time.

- Price range.

- Need for sleeping accommodations.

After obtaining the above information, contact the Transportation company and make the reservations. Inform your client of the bur number, his seat(s), departure time, location of departure, and estimated arrival time at his destination. Of course, be sure to obtain a confirmation number and provide any additional details your client might require to make his trip safe and enjoyable.

# Reservations for Rail Travel

Railroad travel, like travel by bus and motorcoach, is not likely to be the most important part of your sales, however, the income derived from booking seats on railroads can be noteworthy. To ensure that you meet the needs of clients who wish to travel by rail, create a Client Railroad Data Sheet. Include the following information:

- Client's name.

- Client's address and phone number.

- Number of people in your client's party, noting if any children or seniors will be present. Some railroads offer discounted prices for children and seniors on some routes.

- Destination.

- Place from which they are leaving.

- Departure time and estimated arrival time.

- Need for sleeping accommodations.

Once you have placed the reservation, be sure to confirm the times, places, and seating with your client. Also inform him of any additional information which will help to make his trip more enjoyable.

Booking travel reservations and accommodations for your clients will, without doubt, be the major component of your travel agency's operations. Establishing efficient and accurate protocols for bookings will help you to meet the needs of your clients and will give them a reason to return to you for assistance with their future travel plans.

# Providing Travel Services for Groups

Although booking travel plans and accommodations for groups requires meticulous attention to details, providing group travel services offers you the potential of earning significant commissions. Because you are serving the travel needs of several people at once, there are various personalities with which you must interact and various potential pitfalls you must avoid, however, the rewards can be noteworthy to your overall profits. Indeed, many specialized travel agencies focus their services solely on groups.

The travel agency that offers services to groups is seldom without clients. In some communities the number of groups that require travel services at one time or another is enough to keep travel agencies busy throughout the year. Consider the following as potential group clients:

- Ethnic groups.

- School groups – for example, the German club for a summer trip to Germany or a senior class trip to Disney World.

- Senior citizens groups.

- Community organizations such as the Elks or Kiwanis.

- Special organizations such as the VFW (Veterans of Foreign Wars).

- Your local Little League team when they are traveling to a regional or national site for the Little League World Series.

- Church groups.

- Business organizations.

- Singles groups.

- Recreational clubs.

This is just a partial list and there are doubtless many other potential groups in your community that might require travel services. Moreover, the potential destinations are about as limitless as the potential number of groups you might provide services to. Tour packages of Europe – especially the "old country" for ethnic groups – a cruise through the Caribbean, a week in Australia, Superbowl weekend, or a getaway to Bermuda offer excitement and entertainment to groups.

Since it is likely that many of the groups who regularly travel already have used the services of a travel agency, you will probably need to contact them and offer your services, highlighting how the plans you can arrange are better than those of your competitors. In many cases this is not as difficult a task as it may at first seem. Like most people who travel, the typical group does not have limitless funds and its group leader is looking for efficient and reliable service at the most reasonable prices. This gives you an opportunity to make a sale.

# Finding Groups for Your Travel Services

Many groups that are potential candidates for your travel services are likely to be found in your community. Finding them requires little more than good old-fashioned prospecting.

One of the best places to start is the local newspaper under headings such as "Community Happenings," or "Local Events." Meeting times and special events of numerous groups and organizations are noted in such sections. Once you have the name of the group, you can easily check the phone book or call information for a contact person. In many cases, when groups are mentioned in the newspaper, a phone number or contact person is included, which makes your task of research easier.

Just about any place people gather is potentially a spot where you can learn about groups that might be interested in your travel services. Whenever someone mentions a local or regional group, note the group's name and contact person, if possible, and follow up later with a phone call or mailing.

Before contacting the leader of any group about travel services, however, you should formulate a plan or plans which will probably be of interest to them. Calling cold without specific travel plans is often frowned upon by busy group leaders. For example, if you call your local Polish-American club and simply tell them you are a travel agent who can manage their travel needs, you are likely to receive a polite thank-you with the comment that they will call if they need travel services. However, if you call and explain that you are offering a special tour of Poland and Europe at excellent rates, you will probably spark interest. Always offer to come by and discuss your travel plans in greater detail. Formulating specific travel plans for the various groups you intend to approach is essential if you are to be successful in selling to groups. While this reqires research prior to approaching the group leaders, it greatly increases the chances of selling your services.

Along with calling groups and offering travel services, you should also send out flyers and brochures that offer well-conceived travel plans for specific groups. Making just a few phone calls each week and mailing three or four packages can lead to big group sales.

# Selling to Groups

While you will generate interest in your travel agency by telephone contact, most of your sales to groups will be a result of face-to-face selling. After your initial contact, if the group leader is interested, he or she will arrange an appointment with you at which time you will have the opportunity to present your travel options to the group in detail.

When you go for an interview with the leader of any group, always remember that you are attempting to sell your travel services not just to this individual but to several. You must, therefore, always emphasize the practical aspects of your travel plans for the group.

Since the group leader will decide whether or not to present your travel plans to the group at large, you must make a positive impression during this meeting. You should come to the meeting well dressed and in a professional manner. You should have brochures and promotional literature of the travel plans you can offer to the group, including prices. You should also have ready a list of references the group leader can contact and who will attest to your professionalism and expertise. If possible, include references from former groups for whom you have provided travel services.

During your discussion, be sure to mention your experience and particularly any other tours you have arranged. Also note any special services your agency can provide that separate it from your competitors. Stress your commitment to personal service.

As you continue your discussion, ask the group leader questions that will help you to understand any special needs his or her group may have, and especially how you might be able to satisfy those needs. The more information you obtain about the group, the more equipped you will be to formulate acceptable travel options. Following are some important questions:

- How many members does the group have?

- What is the make-up of the general membership? Retirees, mostly young men, mostly singles, etc.?

- Who has the authority to make decisions regarding travel? Presumably it will be the individual to whom you are speaking. If it isn't, you need to know who you should be speaking with. Speaking with those in decision-making positions will help speed your way to sales.

- Do any of the members have special needs for traveling? Special needs of some members can affect your travel arrangements.

- What, if any, other group tours or trips, members of the group have participated in? Also ask what their experiences were. If they were dissatisfied with any part of the trip, try to find out why they were displeased and explain how you can prevent such problems from occurring on trips you arrange.

- Ask what type of travel group members prefer – tours, cruises, resort stays, etc. Try to find out what type of accommodations members prefer, and what type of amenities they like to have. Ask what types of special events they enjoy.

- Find out if any trips group members are considering in the future. Offer to provide a proposal of your own. Perhaps you can offer the same or a similar trip at better rates. If you can't beat the rates of your competitor, perhaps you can provide more service.

It is unlikely that you will sell a travel package to the leader of a group at the first meeting. Most likely you will need to contact the group again. Always send a follow-up note after your initial meeting, and then periodic reminders of your travel agency's willingness to provide specialized services to the group. Include brochures and promotional literature with your mailings, and emphasize your willingness to bid on any trip group members wish to make.

An effective way to ensure that your agency has a fair chance of securing a group's travel business is to request that group leaders present you with their requirements for their trip. Preferably, this will be a data sheet that all interested travel agencies will receive. Written requirements puts all agencies on equal footing and helps to ensure that the agency with the best overall offer and service will obtain the group's business. Whenever you receive a sheet of requirements detailing a group's travel preferences, formulate the best deal you can based on upon the number of group members, flight or cruise plans, locations, accommodations, meal plans, events and celebrations, and shopping and special activities.

For most groups, you will probably pitch your proposal to a committee comprised of anywhere from three to several people. Go before the committee prepared with specifics regarding the proposed trip. Try to find out in advance how many people you will be speaking to and create a folder of travel materials for each. A carefully planned daily itinerary of stops, stays, and events will impress committee members with your expertise and thoroughness and will capture their attention for your presentation. To further enhance your presentation, a short video or slide show can help your audience visualize the places of which you are speaking. (Many travel service providers such as airlines and resorts can provide you with videos of favorite vacation spots and sightseeing tours, either free or for a nominal cost.) Strive to include all pertinent information in your presentation. Finally, always provide plenty of promotional literature and brochures.

At the conclusion of your presentation, answer any questions your audience may have with as much detail as you can. Emphasize that you are willing to tailor your trip proposal to the needs of the group and entertain any special requests. Keep in mind that the members of the group will not only be sold on the trip you are offering, but on you, as well. Travel agents who they perceive as being knowledgeable, trustworthy, and considerate of the group's needs have already passed major obstacles in their attempt at a sale.

# Determining the Price of a Group Trip

Because group trips usually are comprised of many individuals, the potential for a high profit margin is excellent. Unfortunately, if things go wrong, the reverse is also true. You must, therefore, pay meticulous attention to the details and costs in determining the prices you will charge for group trips. You must consider every part and aspect of the tour, balancing costs and price and making certain that you have an acceptable profit.

For some group trips, you will package the entire itinerary, while for others you will work with other travel providers. Whichever way the trip is designed, costs should never be underestimated. Underestimating your costs erodes your profit margins and can in time lead to the bankruptcy of your agency.

Most importantly, you must estimate the potential numbers of travelers accurately. Perhaps the group has a total membership of 120, and you estimate that 50 of them will be interested in your travel proposal. After all, this is less than half of the group's membership, and so you establish your price and make arrangements with tour operators for a travel party of 50. When the reservations come in, however, you receive only 25 commitments. This places you in the uncomfortable position of going ahead with the trip and operating at a loss, canceling, or asking the participants for more money. None is a good option, for each casts your agency in a poor light and reflects negatively on your expertise.

To avoid this situation, always figure your costs from a conservative estimate of the number of people you expect to participate. Of course, while doing so, you need to be cognizant of the prices of other travel agencies and make every effort to remain competitive. Another step to take is to insert a clause in the contract that the price quoted is based on a specific number of travelers, and that if the participants fall below that number the cost of the trip per individual increases.

If more people than you expect sign on for the trip, you will realize greater profits as the cost of the tour per person will decrease. Under such conditions, tour operators typically bill the travel agency less per person. You have several options for this extra money. You may simply receive it as an increased profit margin, you may refund some or all of the extra money to your clients, or you may purchase some additional services or activities for the trip.

Accurate pricing for group trips is essential. Even small oversights, for example, a short visit to a site off the main program can result in big differences between cost estimates and actual expenses. When working up prices, you must account for every expense. Be sure to obtain written confirmation of prices from service providers, and remember to figure in the differences between American dollars and local currencies. Ignoring exchange rates can radically affect your estimates.

When figuring costs, always consider the following:

- Transportation costs, including airfare, cruise fees, bus fees, rail tickets, etc.

- Transfers.

- Accommodations, including all stays.

- Baggage handling.

- Meals.

- Entrance fees.

- Special costs, perhaps for a local celebration or event.

- Taxes.

- Tips.

- Costs for tour managers or local guides.

- Exchange rate.

These are just some of the many costs you may encounter when pricing a trip for a group. Along with costs for the actual trip, you must estimate costs associated with the trip. In pricing, also estimate costs for your time in meeting with group members, creating and printing promotional materials, advertising, phone usage, staff, and postage. Try to account for everything; any cost you overlook will likely need to be deducted from your profits.

Many agencies typically add a 15% markup to their total anticipated costs. This markup should then cover the costs and provide a profit. Depending upon your competition, a 15% markup may be too high and you might need to lower it perhaps to 12%. While a lower markup will have a better chance of obtaining business, it leaves you with a smaller margin if you have omitted any costs. In some cases, especially where the competition is not as strong, or the area's population is affluent, you might be able to increase your markup to 20%, but you must remain competitively priced. Often, if you provide personal service that goes beyond the service offered by other agencies, you may be able to price your services slightly higher than your competitors and still attract business.

# Avoiding Underpricing

When pricing group tours and travel packages, many new travel agencies underprice their competitors in an attempt of gaining business. This is a risky strategy. While they may attract new clients quickly, they may be so severely undermining their profit margin that the agency has little earnings. Remember the old adage: "It's not how much you make but how much you keep." An agency whose gross income is a half million dollars in the first year of operation is unlikely to stay in business much longer if its operating costs are $498,000 before you take your salary.

Avoid the temptation to market your services below what they are worth, and less than you need to earn a fair profit and salary. A good way to price your services fairly and accurately is to regularly check the prices of your competitors for similar services. If your competitors are marketing similar travel packages and services for considerably more than you are, then you are clearly priced too low. Even attaining a high volume will not enable you to achieve profitability. If, on the other hand, the prices of your competitors are well below yours, your prices are too high. In either case you should adjust your prices.

There will also be times when you present a client with a price for a trip, and he makes a counter offer. This is not uncommon when marketing to groups who will often attempt to find the best price for their trips. Knowing that they are offering several potential travelers emboldens them to ask for the lowest rates possible. When this happens, assess your costs and projected earnings from the proposed trip carefully. You may find that reducing your price will undermine your profits so that the trip is not worth your efforts. In this case,

171

you should pass on the trip. Explain to the client that you are unable to meet his price, but that you will welcome the opportunity to offer a travel proposal in the future.

From time to time, you may run a special – perhaps tour operators have reduced their prices and you can pass those savings on to your clients – or you may offer a discount to increase business. These are fine strategies, but you should use them with caution. If you offer too many discounts, clients will come to think that your ordinary prices are too high and unfair. They may begin to wait for the next discount before planning their next trip. For many travel agencies, the discount is best used with long-term travel arrangements that will result in repeated business. Perhaps a local business organization regularly sends some of its members on fact-finding trips or seminars, and a discount can secure their business for an entire year.

# Working with Tour Leaders

There will be times that individuals who can gather groups for travel will contact you about a group tour. These "leaders" – which might be the president of a community group, a teacher, or even a church official – will usually promise 15, 20, or more people for a trip that you would arrange. For his efforts, the tour leader expects to travel for free.

While this may sound like a wonderful opportunity for business, you should exercise both discretion and caution before committing to any plan. Most importantly, you should determine the true potential of the so-called leader being able to assemble as many individuals as he has promised. An officer of the local environment club, which has eight members, will probably be hard-pressed to assemble the 30 people he has promised for the trip. On the other hand, the German teacher who believes that ten of his 40 German club members would sign on for a summer tour of Germany can probably deliver those numbers.

You must also evaluate the individual making the offer. Without appearing suspicious, you must ascertain his or her honesty and trustworthiness. You don't want to waste time with dreamers who have grand ideas but little hope of achieving them. Furthermore, because a tour leader will be responsible for the tour's smooth-running, you must select leaders with care. Following are some of a tour leader's responsibilities:

- The tour leader must be capable of dealing with the various individuals that will be a part of his group. The leader, therefore, must possess a strong personality as well as the experience needed to interact with others in novel places and situations.

- The leader should be someone who commands respect from his group.

- The leader should be someone who is capable of managing unforeseen events and problems – lost luggage, missed transfers, transportation breakdowns, illness of a group member, poorly prepared food, etc.

You can reduce the chances for confusion and mishaps by running through a checklist with your tour leader before departure that includes the following:

- A list containing the names of all group members and also someone to contact in case of an emergency.

- Passport numbers.

- Airline ticket numbers.

- Baggage tags and labels.

- Copies of all pertinent documents required for travel, accommodations, etc.

- Room assignments.

- Lists showing special activities and which group members will be attending.

- Copy of tour itinerary.

- Any necessary schedules.

A good way to gauge a so-called tour leader's sincerity is to suggest that he and you jointly assume the costs of promotional materials. If the leader provides the number of travelers he promises, he would be reimbursed for his share of the promotional costs. Only leaders who truly believe that they can bring along enough people to make the trip profitable will accept this offer.

Since many travel service providers do not offer free trips for tour leaders, you will need to include the leader's free travel into your overall cost estimates. In this case, the other travelers are paying for the leader's fare. Some airlines, cruises, and hotels offer discounts and free travel for leaders of large groups, and you should always contact service providers regarding their policies.

Of course, you may assume the role of a tour leader, assemble a group of individuals – perhaps relatives, friends, and neighbors – and organize a tour. In this case, you would travel for free while still earning income for your agency. You must, however, be willing to assume the duties of a tour leader, which can be somewhat demanding.

Arranging trips and tours for groups can be a significant source of income to your travel agency. Although you must plan with care and diligence, accommodating the travel needs of groups can become an important component of your agency's profitability.

# Opportunities in Commercial Travel

Many travel agencies specialize in providing services for businesses, deriving much of their yearly income from this sector of the industry. As more and more companies expand their markets domestically and internationally, this market will grow, adding handsomely to the profits of travel agencies. By securing the business of corporate clients, you will be helping to secure your agency's future.

Before you promote your services to companies, however, you must determine if this is the type of business you wish to pursue. Business travelers offer your agency opportunity, but they are demanding in the level and quality of the services they expect. Following is a summary of the benefits and potential pitfalls of working with corporate clients.

First, the benefits –

- Corporations can provide a steady flow of repeat clients. Managing the travel needs of just a few large corporate clients can account for the major part of a small travel agency's business.

- Business travelers fly frequently. Most are experienced travelers and have little difficulty making their flights and finding their hotels. It is less likely for a corporate client to call you because he has gotten lost and missed his flight than for a vacationer to call after watching his plane leave from the wrong gate.

- In an effort to reduce their costs, many companies rely on agencies to make the travel arrangements for their personnel. This results in potential business for you.

- When business travelers are satisfied with your services for their company, they will often turn to you to arrange their personal trips.

The potential pitfalls –

- Corporate clients can be demanding. Most will expect high quality services at the lowest possible prices. Corporate executives are not hesitant to bargain, and you must know precisely how low you can set your price before you begin negotiations. It is easy to make a low offer to obtain business only to realize later that you have denied yourself a fair profit.

- Corporate clients do not hesitate to switch their business when the opportunity arises. There is little loyalty when price is the most important factor. Avoid becoming overly dependent on any company. If you unexpectedly lose their business, you will still have other sources of income.

- Business travelers can be somewhat finicky. Depending upon their customers, they may need travel arrangements to be made on short notice, or they may change plans on equally short notice. You must be prepared to manage travel plans in fluctuating conditions, often with tight deadlines. Your office operations must be geared to handle abrupt changes in plans.

- Some companies are chronic late-payers. Unlike the typical vacationer who pays his travel costs with a credit card, many companies that are heavy users of travel services prefer to pay their bills on a set schedule. When that schedule becomes disrupted – or if paying their travel agent is not a high priority – your income will suffer. You must prepared to cover your costs in such circumstances. You must also be ready to curtail business with companies that are habitually late with payment. This can sometimes be a hard decision to make, especially if the company represents a big account. Consequently, small agencies will often overlook late payments if the company provides a high volume of business. This is a trap you should avoid, however, because in

179

the end the disruption to your cash flow and the time you spend pursuing payment will undermine your overall operations.

- Major corporations that offer heavy volume will come to expect prompt service. This may put you in a position where you must delay other business to handle your corporate client. This may lead to the loss of other business.

- Corporate executives expect top professionalism from travel agents. The manner with which you arrange travel plans for a friend or neighbor will likely be insufficient for the high-level business executive. You should have accumulated a solid measure of experience before approaching business leaders about your travel services.

- If your corporate accounts grow, you may need to hire additional staff. This may require an investment in a new office and new equipment. You must be sure that once you expand you will retain your corporate accounts.

- The competition for business accounts can be high, and you may find yourself cutting prices to the pint where your profit margin is severely reduced.

If you feel that selling travel services tocorporations is an opportunity that you would enjoy, you must develop a marketing plan that addresses the needs of business travelers. Keep in mind that the needs of the business traveler are different than those of the vacationer or the couple heading off to a weekend getaway. Most importantly, the business traveler has "business" on his mind, and anything you do that will help make his trip easier and more effective will be greatly appreciated. Get him to his destination city in plenty of time for his meeting and he will remember your competence. Have him arrive a half-hour before the meeting begins, and he will dismiss you as an amateur and probably not use your services again.

## Marketing Your Services to Business Travelers

When marketing the services of your travel agency to business executives, it is necessary that they perceive you as being an agent who values corporate clients. Even if you provide a variety of services to the general public, it should be clear that a major focus of your agency is the business traveler.

Before contacting company leaders, develop a marketing plan. While you may not know the company's precise travel needs, you should possess a firm idea of the services you can offer. If the client asks you to submit an offer for a specific trip, be ready to do so as quickly as possible. Be thorough, however, and don't sacrifice accuracy for speed. Figure in all costs and know what your bottom price is. No matter how much you might like to secure the company's business, avoid making an offer that leaves you with an inadequate profit margin.

When promoting your travel services to companies, consider the following:

- Emphasize how your agency is different from your competitors. In particular note any special benefits such as personalized service, free delivery of tickets, or an informative website that permits clients to easily obtain vital information.

- Develop a strong promotional plan aimed at business clients. Build a list of potential clients by consulting the Yellow Pages, business and association directories, your local Chamber of Commerce, the business section of local newspapers, friends and colleagues. Since most companies will not be interested in your services – they may not require the use of a travel agent or they may already have one – you need to approach as many companies as you can.

- Contact potential clients by phone. When calling, ask to speak with the person responsible for the company's travel needs. Try to speak only with this person, for it is likely that he or she will be the one who has the authority to make travel decisions.

- Send promotional packages, explaining who you are and detailing the travel services that you offer. Emphasize the advantages you can provide that separate you from your competitors. In your mailing, express your willingness to present a bid on the company's next trip. A week or so after the mailing, call and speak with the company's travel officer.

- Find out if the company has a travel policy. If they do, ask if they can send you a copy and then formulate a proposal that satisfies their guidelines.

- Set up appointments and meet with company officials in person. A face-to-face meeting gives you the opportunity to fully explain the services you offer.

- Find out as much as you can about your potential clients and design travel services that will satisfy their needs.

- Always treat business clients as individuals and not as mere representatives of the company. As with any potential client, ascertain their specific needs and strive to satisfy them.

Even though your major goal may be to provide travel services for companies, you can also derive much personal travel business from corporate accounts. When business clients realize that you make their trips easier and more enjoyable, they will be inclined to have you book their personal travel plans. Without appearing overzealous in your marketing efforts, always make certain that business clients know that you are willing to manage all of their professional and personal travel plans. This additional business can add significantly to your earnings.

# Using Your Travel Agency as a Stepping Stone to Global Entrepreneuring

Most people who become travel agents view their agency as an investment and a business. Along with enjoying the monetary benefits of a profitable travel agency, many agents also take advantage of the industry's perks – namely the deep discounts on travel services one can receive for simply being an agent who directs business to travel providers. There are many interesting opportunities.

As a travel agent, you almost certainly will be offered "familiarization tours" by cruise lines and tour operators. Such tours are usually reduced in cost and sometimes are free. If you direct many travelers to a particular destination and use the same airline, you may be offered special trips. Of course, the drawback is that most of these trips are offered at times convenient to the provider. You will need to be flexible in your schedule and plans to be able to take advantage of such trips, however, the trips themselves can be a delightful experience. You may, for example, be able to go on a 10-day familiarization tour of Europe at the deeply discounted price of a few hundred dollars. Not only can you enjoy yourself, you can see the continent and broaden your travel experiences, which you can then use to attract new clients. After all, who can speak with more authority about a European tour than a travel agent who went on that very tour?

While free and reduced travel are major benefits of owning a travel agency, there is another, less well known, benefit that few agents consider – global entrepreneuring. A global entrepreneur is, essentially, an investor who views the entire world as a place of possible investment. Global investors may own securities in a tax haven in the Caribbean, may protect their assets in a trust in Seychelles, or may invest in a local company in Madeira where they can take advantage of business-friendly tax laws. The global investor views investment opportunities as limitless because he sees investment on a worldwide scale.

The travel agent who uses familiarization tours and discounted trips as a means with which to identify potential investment opportunities enjoys a significant advantage over the individual who considers overseas investments only through news reports, company information, and articles in journals and newspapers. Visiting the sites of potential investment is perhaps the best way to ascertain an investment's overall potential. Being able to see the locality, speak with the people associated with the company, and gain first-hand knowledge of the business climate of the region go far beyond the information that can be gleaned from other sources.

For the travel agent who wishes to pursue global investing, the benefits of his agency in permitting him to research potential investments while traveling are hard to equal. It seldom becomes a case of searching fruitlessly for possible investments, as most global investors find that the scope of investment opportunities are as vast as the world itself.

## Guidelines for Global Investing

Just like any type of investing, successful global investing requires meticulous research, accurate information, scrupulous evaluation, and precise decision-making. Because you will be dealing with individuals and companies located in other countries, whose business practices, laws, and traditions may be unfamiliar, you must be cautious, while at the same time maintaining an open mind about the potential of specific investments. Dealing with foreign cultures demands that you take the steps to understand the culture. Following are some cautions that should not be ignored:

- Learn as much about the country in which you are considering investment. This includes the political system, business laws and practices – particularly those that affect foreigners – tax system, and investment procedures. Many countries around the world welcome and encourage foreign investment and have created agencies who staff can facilitate investment.

- Contact the country's embassy and ask for information about investment.

- Realize that most North Americans generally feel more comfortable investing in places where English is spoken and English tradition and laws are common. This happens to include many prime investment sites.

- Become knowledgeable about global investing. Pay attention to financial news, read investment journals and newsletters, and keep aware of economic trends and fluctuations. Become an expert in investment on the global scale. When you travel to investment sites, compare what you witness with what you already know.

- Obtain specific information about investment options and companies.

- When you travel to countries in which you are considering investing, visit specific companies and sites. You should have a list of questions to ask regarding the investment, especially regarding investment by foreigners. If anything makes you uncomfortable – the facilities, staff, or general area – you would be wise to pass on the investment and consider another.

- Before investing and before signing any contracts, agreements, etc., have your attorney review them carefully. Ideally, your attorney should have experience with international business practices.

As the world's economy expands and the business ties between countries tighten, investing exclusively in American companies no longer guarantees the best and safest returns. The global economy is the economy of the future and those who take equity positions in it early are the ones who will profit most handsomely. Using your travel benefits gives you a powerful advantage, for you can travel virtually free to various parts of the world seeking the most lucrative investment options.

# Worldwide Investment Opportunities

Global investment opportunities abound. From investing in securities in jurisdictions known as tax havens – where laws are designed to limit one's tax exposure and protect assets – to investing in local companies or establishing new ones in lands that welcome business and have enacted laws favorable to business, investors can pick from among countless investment options. The upcoming pages examine ten of the best sites for global investing. There are many, many more.

## Barbados

Barbados is a delightful tourist destination in the West Indies. The island, however, is far more than a vacation paradise. In an effort to build the island's economic base, the government has enacted a variety of laws that offer numerous incentives for new businesses whose operations center around information and financial services or manufacturing.

Following are the major incentives for companies that provide information services:

- A tax rate of 2.5% for companies that operate internationally.

- Exemptions from import tariffs on equipment necessary for production.

- The possibility of an accelerated allowance for depreciation.

Barbados also offers numerous incentives for manufacturing companies in export industries, the most significant of which include:

- A tax rate of 2.5% for companies that operate internationally.

- Exemptions from import tariffs on equipment necessary for production.

- The possibility of an accelerated allowance for depreciation.

Barbados also offers numerous incentives for manufacturing companies in export industries, the most significant of which include:

- An exemption from taxes for up to ten years on corporate profits.

- Once the exemption period is done, export companies may qualify for a tax rate of 2.5%.

- Companies may qualify for exemptions from certain import duties, including duties on equipment parts, production machinery, and raw materials.

International service companies are also eligible for incentives, including:

- A tax exemption for U.S. foreign sales corporations.

- A tax exemption for "captive insurance companies."

- Tax rates of 1 to 2.5% on the profits of investment companies.

- A tax rate of 2.5% for international business companies.

- A tax rate of 2.5% on the profits of information technology service companies.

Foreign investors also enjoy impressive incentives under the law in Barbados, including:

- A maximum tax rate of 2.5% on profits.

- Exemptions from local taxes on dividends, interests, fees, royalties, management fees, and other incomes.

- Exemptions from taxes and duties on machinery, raw materials, and goods imported into Barbados.

- An exemption from filing public financial statements.

- An exemption from exchange controls.

- Benefits guaranteed for 15 years.

## The Cayman Islands

A dependency of Great Britain, the Cayman Islands are located in the Caribbean Sea, splitting the distance between

Cuba and Honduras. Tourism – about one million visitors a year – and an offshore financial center are the foundation of an economy that has resulted in the islands' citizens enjoying one of the highest living standards in the world.

The financial system on the Cayman Islands offers investors myriad investment options. An added benefit is the tax code, in which there is no income tax or direct taxation of any kind. Investments on the islands can provide a greater return than in jurisdictions where earnings are taxed.

## Puerto Rico

Puerto Rico, often referred to as an economic jewel in the Caribbean, has the third highest per capita income in the Western Hemisphere after the U.S. and Canada. The strength of the island's economy is based on several factors: its close relationship with the U.S., competent planning on the part of island officials, and tax laws designed to attract business.

Two of the island's most attractive incentives center around federal tax exemptions. Under Section 9 of the Federal Relations Act, individuals or corporations in Puerto Rico are not subject to U.S. Internal Revenue Service laws. In addition, under Section 936 of the U.S. Internal Revenue Code, corporate profits earned in Puerto Rico are favored by federal tax credits after profits are remitted to U.S. Parent companies.

Other incentives for investors include:

- A 90% exemption from Puerto Rico taxes is possible for service industries and manufacturers. Eligible companies may enjoy these exemptions from 10 to 25 years, depending upon their location.

- A 60% exemption from municipal fees, excise, and various taxes for licenses is possible for companies.

- Tax-exempt years may be deferred, giving companies the flexibility to pay tax during those years when their taxable earnings are low.

- Tax-exemption agreements are protected by both the U.S. Constitution and the Constitution of Puerto Rico.

Through the Tourism Development Law, the government of Puerto Rico provides several incentives to investors, including:

- Projects that fall within the parameters of the law are eligible for a ten-year exemption from various

195

island taxes. The exemptions may be renewed for an additional ten-year period.

- Income and dividends from tourist-related projects are eligible for a 90% exemption from tax.

- For eligible tourism projects, the law provides for a 50% tax credit for investments.

In addition to the noted incentives, Puerto Rico has two foreign trade zones – one in Mayaguez and the other in San Juan. These zones confer various benefits on companies operating within them. Because the zones are considered to be outside of U.S. Customs, but within Puerto Rico, firms operating within them enjoy the jurisdiction of the U.S. yet conduct their business in the manner of Puerto Rican exporters. Companies also enjoy an export manufacturing exemption (available for a ten-year period). Essentially all this provides a company with a tax-free, duty-free base within the jurisdiction of the U.S. This is perhaps one of the most advantageous exporting positions in the world.

## Madeira

The Madeira Islands, of which the island of Madeira is the largest, are located in the east Atlantic Ocean. Although the islands are officially a part of the Portuguese district of Funchal, they enjoy much autonomy. This autonomy has resulted in the government of the islands enacting numerous laws providing incentive to investment.

Some of Madeira's most significant incentives are found in the island's industrial free trade zone. Major companies from Europe, South America, and Africa operate in the zone, which welcomes all types of industrial activity. Of the zones many incentives, the most important include:

- An exemption until 2011 from corporate income taxes on income derived from business in the zone.

- An exemption from municipal property taxes on income derived from business carried out in the zone.

- Exemptions from local taxes.

- Exemptions from transfer taxes, gift taxes, and inheritance taxes under certain conditions.

- An exemption from taxes on capital gains on the sales of fixed assets.

- An exemption from having to withhold tax from interest on loans, from foreign banks, and on bonds issued by companies.

- An exemption from having to withhold taxes from the payment of royalties.

- An exemption from export quotas.

- An exemption from VAT and custom duties on imported goods, stored and/or transferred in the zone.

Individuals also may benefit from special incentives including:

- An exemption from withholding and income tax on dividends, interest on loans of shareholders, and other types of income received by investors in companies operating in the zone.

- An exemption from inheritance, gift, and transfer tax in regard to all transfers of shares in the capital of companies operating exclusively in the zone.

In recent years Madeira has evolved as an offshore financial center and consequently offers incentives in this sector, including:

- An exemption for offshore entities from corporate taxes on all revenues obtained from operations conducted by the branch office.

- An exemption for offshore entities from withholding taxes on revenues paid by branches in the funding of other operations.

- An exemption for international branches from withholding taxes on revenues that are paid by international branches in the funding of other operations.

The above exemptions are based on the condition that these activities are conducted exclusively with non-residents in Portuguese territory or with other entities established legally within the framework of the free trade zone. Nonetheless, they are powerful incentives.

International service companies – including consulting, management, trading, holding, and trust – also enjoy numerous incentives in Madeira, including:

- An exemption from corporate taxes on income derived from shares in other companies, as long as they are established within the legal framework of the International Business Center of Madeira and/or are located outside the territory of the EU. The exemption runs until 2011.

- A tax exemption on the interests of loans contracted by entities that are legally licensed within the framework of Madeira's International Business Center. This exemption is contingent on the fact that the loans are used for operations within the legal framework, and the lenders are non-residents in Portuguese territory.

- An exemption for non-resident shareholders from corporate and individual taxes on dividends derived from the income of the entities in which they hold shares. The exemption runs until 2011, provided the operations of the entities remain within the legal framework of the International Business Center.

## The Republic of Ireland

The Republic of Ireland, usually referred to as simply Ireland, offers a variety of investment opportunities. In an effort to support the island's economy, the government has enacted legislation fostering an investment climate.

Within the last decade, Ireland has developed into one of Europe's most important financial centers. Indeed, many of the nation's incentives focus on the financial services sector, including:

- A 10% tax rate on profits from eligible business activities.

- An exemption from local property taxes for a period of ten years.

- A write-off of 100% for expenditures for new equipment during the first year of operation.

- A write-off of 100% for the costs of new facilities during the first year for owners who occupy their sites.

- A write-off of 54% for new building costs in the first year for lessors and a write-off of the balance at 4% per annum in following years.

Companies whose operations primarily focus on manufacturing enjoy a special 10% corporate tax rate. Both resident and non-resident companies conducting their business in Ireland through a branch may be eligible for this rate. Many companies enjoy this special rate until the year 2010.

## Malta

The Maltese Islands occupy an enviable location near the center of the Mediterranean Sea between Italy and North Africa. Malta, which is the principal island of a group, benefits from a high volume of trade because of its location as well as legislation that has created a friendly business climate.

Investors can take advantage of many incentives, the most significant of which include:

- A tax holiday of ten years for companies that are 95% or more export-oriented.

- An exemption for eligible companies from local and municipal taxes.

- The availability of investment tax credits.

- An accelerated rate of allowances for depreciation.

- Special loans at extremely low rates for investment in new facilities, machinery, and fixed assets.

- Duty-free importation of materials when used in export products.

- Duty-free shipment on various products shipped to the EC.

- Reduced tariffs on products targeted for export to the U.S.

## St. Kitts and Nevis

Located between Puerto Rico, Trinidad, and Tobago, the two-island nation of St. Kitts and Nevis provides exceptional investment opportunities. One of the best sites for asset protection trusts in the world (Nevis), combined with numerous impressive incentives, makes these islands a primary spot for investors. Following are the most important investment incentives:

- No personal income taxes on the islands.

- No gift taxes, sales tax, or estate duties.

- Corporate tax holidays may be granted for periods from ten to 15 years.

- Corporate tax holidays for "enclave" industries – companies that produce goods exclusively for export outside of the CARICOM region, may be granted to eligible companies for periods of up to 15 years.

- Companies can qualify for an exemption from import duties on parts, production and raw materials.

- Hotel owners can enjoy substantial benefits from the Hotel Aids Ordinance. Under the ordinance's provisions, the profits of a hotel of more than 30 bedrooms is exempt from income tax for a period of ten years. Hotels of fewer rooms may qualify for exemptions for up to five years.

## Seychelles

Seychelles is an archipelago of some 118 islands and islets located in the Indian Ocean, northeast of Madagascar. In recent years, the government has enacted legislation that has transformed the islands into a valuable site for investment. This is particularly true of Seychelles's laws governing international trusts, which are among the safest and most effective in the world. In addition, numerous incentives make the islands an attractive site for investment, the most important of which include:

- No personal income tax.

- No withholding tax on dividends.

- Accelerated rates of depreciation.

- No wealth tax, gift tax, property tax, capital gains tax, death duties, or taxes on property.

- No import duties on capital equipment.

- A low tax rate of 15% for businesses. Additional tax credits may result in the overall effective rate being reduced to 9%.

- In some industries, some companies may be eligible for long-term tax holidays.

**Singapore**

Located within one of the world's most dynamic economic regions, the Republic of Singapore is well positioned to benefit from international commerce. Its pro-business environment and powerful incentives have combined to give its residents one of the highest standards of living in the world.

To encourage investors to establish businesses in Singapore, the government offers the following inducements:

- For up to ten years, an exemption of corporate taxes on income that results from pioneer activity.

- A tax rate of as low as 10% on income from specific, qualifying activities. This special rate may last for up to ten years.

- For companies that expand their operations, an exemption from corporate tax on income that exceeds pre-expansion levels for a period up to five years.

- A tax rate of 10% on income that is derived from the provision of approved services in Singapore.

206

The period may last for ten years with extensions possible.

- A possible full exemption of withholding tax on approved royalties.

- A possible full exemption of withholding tax on interest payments.

- An exemption of corporate tax on 90% of qualifying export income. The period for this exemption is typically five years, but it may be extended.

## Switzerland

Few can argue that Switzerland is the global investment capital of the world. Investors have a choice of thousands of investment options, which Swiss investment firms will gladly and competently manage. Indeed, it is the Swiss reputation for financial responsibility, integrity, and security that attract investors from around the world.

Of the many benefits and advantages Switzerland offers investors, perhaps the following are the most significant:

- The Swiss franc is perhaps the most solid currency in the world, backed 100% by gold.

- Switzerland has a long history of fiscal responsibility. Institutions and laws support a steady, secure, and professional financial environment.

- Switzerland has a strong tradition of respecting confidentiality. Clear privacy laws protect the investors.

The Swiss financial system is built upon the strength of its banks. Considered by many financial experts to be among the world's leaders, Swiss banks offer various services, including deposits and checking, commercial lending, investment services, stock brokerage, and financial planning. The staffs of most Swiss banks have personnel fluent in English, and their knowledge of international finance is broad. Swiss banks can handle the needs of virtually all investors, whether the investor maintains a large or small portfolio. For securities investment on a worldwide scale, Swiss experience and expertise make the nation a leading global investment site.

## Investing throughout the World

As a travel agent, you will enjoy trips at greatly reduced prices, and in some cases, for no cost at all. You can utilize such travel opportunities not only as a means of gaining knowledge and experience which you can share with potential clients, but also as a method of exploring investment opportunities throughout the world. When you go on a familiarization tour of Europe, for example, there is no reason why you can't spend some time in Switzerland exploring possible investments. Of course, you will need to complete the tour, and pay heed to the tour operator's program, for, after all, this is a familiarization tour, but there will be some free time which you can put to use seeking potential investments. A trip to the Cayman Islands, for example, will surely provide you with the chance to investigate investment options there. A free flight that you take to Nevis can enable you to learn about asset protection trusts and how such a trust might be of benefit to your holdings.

The travel agent of today should not limit his view of his agency. He should not think of it as simply providing him with an occupation and an income. The modern travel agent should look upon his agency as a company that offers various opportunities, including traveling the world as an entrepreneur in search of unique, interesting, and profitable investments.

# About the Author

Over the past 25 years, Adam Starchild has been the author of over two dozen books, and hundreds of magazine articles, primarily on business and finance. His articles have appeared in a wide range of publications around the world -- including Business Credit, Euromoney, Finance, The Financial Planner, International Living, Offshore Financial Review, Reason, Tax Planning International, The Bull & Bear, Trust & Estates, and many more.

Now semi-retired, he was the president of an international consulting group specializing in banking, finance and the development of new businesses, including tourist enterprises. He has owned and operated travel agencies, travel wholesalers, and tour operators.

Although this formidable testimony to expertise in his field, plus his current preoccupation with other books-in-progress, would not seem to leave time for a well-rounded existence, Starchild has won two Presidential Sports Awards and written several cookbooks, and is currently involved in a number of personal charitable projects.

His personal website is at http://www.adamstarchild.com/